THE JUDAIC NATURE OF
ISRAELI THEATRE

Contemporary Theatre Studies

A series of books edited by Franc Chamberlain, Nene College, Northampton, UK

Please see the back of this book for other titles in the Contemporary Theatre Studies series

THE JUDAIC NATURE OF ISRAELI THEATRE
A SEARCH FOR IDENTITY

Dan Urian
Tel Aviv University, Israel

Translated by Naomi Paz
Tel Aviv University, Israel

harwood academic publishers
Australia • Canada • France • Germany • India
Japan • Luxembourg • Malaysia • The Netherlands
Russia • Singapore • Switzerland

Amsteldijk 166
1st Floor
1079 LH Amsterdam
The Netherlands

British Library Cataloguing in Publication Data

Urian, Dan
    The Judaic nature of Israeli theatre: a search for
    identity. – (Contemporary theatre studies; v. 31)
    1. Theatre and society – Israel   2. Theatre – Israel –
    Religious aspects – Judaism
    I. Title
    792'.095694

    ISBN 90-5755-056-3

Cover illustration: *Bimah*. Modern deconstruction by Hadass Ophrat of the Abuhav Synagogue in Zefat, built at the beginning of the 16th century. Displayed in 1993 at the Genia Schreiber University Art Gallery, Tel Aviv University. Curator: Prof. Mordechai Omer. Photo: Avraham Hai.

CONTENTS

INTRODUCTION TO THE SERIES

Contemporary Theatre Studies is a book series of special interest to everyone involved in theatre. It consists of monographs on influential figures, studies of movements and ideas in theatre, as well as primary material consisting of theatre-related documents, performing editions of plays in English, and English translations of plays from various vital theatre traditions worldwide.

Franc Chamberlain

ACKNOWLEDGEMENTS

Acknowledgement is made to the following journals for permission to use material that originally appeared in different settings: *Bamah, Assaph* and *Israel Affairs*.

I would like to thank Dwora Gilula, editor of *Bamah*, Eli Rozik, editor of *Assaph* and Efraim Karsh, editor of *Israel Affairs*, whose comments and editorial work greatly assisted me; and Franc Chamberlain, whose sensible and sensitive advice guided me in shaping the final result.

My special thanks to Naomi Paz, who translated and edited the book.

D. U.

LIST OF PLATES
(Between pages 80 and 81)

1. A mask of Rabbi Avraham Shapira, a well-known religious politician, used in the dance prologue to *Tartuffe*, adapted by Yehoshua Sobol and directed by Gedalia Besser at the Haifa Municipal Theatre, 1985.
2. *Status Quo Vadis* by Yehoshua Sobol, directed by Edna Shavit at the Haifa Municipal Theatre, 1973. From right to left: Gedalia Besser, Gita Munte, Yossef Bashi, Ilan Dar, Ilan Toren and Ruth Segal.
3. Shmuel Hasfari's *Kiddush*, directed by Hasfari, at the Cameri Theatre, 1985. From right to left: Dov Navon, Yossi Graber, Edna Fliedel.
4. Yossef Carmon as the Butcher forced to convert to ultra-Orthodoxy, with Yossi Kantz as Hund, in Igal Even-Or's *Fleischer* directed by Amit Gazit at the Cameri Theatre, 1993.
5. *Ish Hassid Haya* by Dan Almagor, directed by Yossi Yzraely, Bimot Theatre, 1968. From right to left: Danny Litany, Batia Barak, Deborah Dotan, Lolik Levy, Shlomo Nizan and Hanna Roth.
6. *Bruria* by Aliza Elion-Israeli, directed by Joyce Miller, Theatre Company of Jerusalem, 1982. Gabriella Lev and Ruth Wieder.
7. *A Night at the Mall* by Orli Castel-Bloom, directed by Oded Kotler, Haifa Municipal Theatre, 1994. A religious married couple of settlers are trapped in the mall, the "palace" of secular and hedonistic Israeli culture. Shragit Bikovsky and Yoav Heit.
8. *Mirkam*, directed by Zippora Luria, Samaria community centre, 1994:
   (a) The opening scene;
   (b) The final monologue by Deborah Recanati;
   (c) An audience of religious women only.
9. Religious stand-up comedy: Noya Shuster and Nurit Hadar in *Bidur K'Halacha*, directed by Hanan Goldblat, 1994.
10. *Nashim b'Yarok* (*Women in Green*).
11. *Boochie* by Yossef Bar-Yossef, directed by Gedalia Besser, Haifa Municipal Theatre, 1984. Yossi Polak (left) as Boochie and Michael Kfir as his father.
12. Uri Zohar and Hanna Laslow in the film *Save the Lifeguard*, screenplay and direction by Uri Zohar, 1977. This was Zohar's last film, before his conversion to ultra-Orthodoxy.
13. Rabbi Uri Zohar proselytizing.
14. Rabbi Benji Levene has performed *The Four Faces of Israel* since 1978.

INTRODUCTION

The question of the Judaic nature of Israeli-Hebrew theatre, and that of the place of Judaism in Israeli culture, are part of the ambivalent identity that characterizes the Israeli immigrant culture which, despite attempts at unification, incorporates several sub-cultures, "and their contrasts," writes Eliezer Schweid, "are great enough to mask their shared features."[1] These contrasts are reflected in the totally opposite viewpoints held by different groups regarding the place of Judaism as culture and religion in the State of Israel.

A discussion of the Jewish aspects of Israeli theatre demands several theoretical and methodological assumptions, the most important of which refers to the theatre as representing a social experience. It is accepted that theatre does not reflect any given reality, but fashions it to its own particular needs. Despite, or perhaps even because of this, however, the ties between theatre and social reality enable the uncovering of both hidden conflicts and overt dissension. The sociologist Georges Gurvich notes the ability of the theatre to give expression to what is otherwise repressed:

> We go to the theatre in order to experience certain social situations which have occasionally been oppressive, and to free ourselves from that oppressiveness [...] what we find at the theatre, when driven there by the problem of real social life, is – all kinds of novel perspectives.[2]

Patrice Pavis too refers to the theatrical text as a document deriving from a hidden social reality. Pavis uses the image of an iceberg to demonstrate the link between theatrical text and the social reality from which it is derived and to which it relates. The visible tip of the iceberg is the text itself. The two concealed parts, below water level, are the "layer" of its intertextual relationships with other texts (not only theatrical) and below them, the ideology at the "base of the iceberg" whose source lies within the social context.[3]

---

[1] Eliezer Schweid, *The Idea of Judaism as Culture*, Tel Aviv, Am Oved, 1995, 314. (Hebrew)

[2] Georges Gurvich, "The Sociology of the Theatre", in: *Sociology of Literature and Drama*, Elizabeth and Tom Burns, (eds.), Harmondsworth, Penguin 1973, 73–74.

[3] Patrice Pavis, "Production et réception au théâtre: la concrétisation du texte dramatique et spectaculaire", *Voix et images de la scène: Vers une sémiologie de la réception*, Lille, Presses Universitaires de Lille, 1985, 288–90.

Zionism is an ideology which fed a culture undergoing renewal; a formerly hegemonic culture, mainly during the period of settlement and after the establishment of the State of Israel (1948). Following election of the first right-wing government in 1977, the status of this culture was questioned, but its centrality was not abolished. The 1996 elections which restored the right-wing and religious parties to power may have totally shattered this hegemony. For about one hundred years the Zionist discourse influenced highbrow Israeli culture (literature, theatre, cinema, the fine arts and music). It ignored the social heterogeneity, economic polarity and the cultural division, alienating itself from the Palestinian, female, religious or oriental "Others". This culture was "supposed to exist side by side", as claimed by Baruch Kimmerling, "as a religion and as a nation, native Israeli and non-native, and Zionism in all its varieties [...] images and ethos were all constructed around the figure of the *chalutz* [pioneer], the *tsabar* [native born Israeli] and the fighter, [...] despite the vastness of this culture and the support provided by the State and its ideological agents (e.g. secular state schools) and even though this culture still stands at the centre of society, it has considerably weakened due to its inability to withstand its own contradictions."[4]

Israeli culture sought ways of presenting a solution to society's conflicts, particularly to the rift between the secular and the religious, between those of western and those of oriental origin, and between Jews and Arabs. This was carried out at first by carefully reproducing the hegemonic status of the secular-western sector of society. The theatre as an institution was one of the tools which served them for this purpose. Problems were raised and "solved" on the theatrical stage, particularly during the first forty years of existence of the State. From the 1980s on, especially during the War in Lebanon (1982–1985), the Hebrew theatre featured biting revelations of hostilities, discords and contradictions, which it presented as insoluble. During the same period, the "mainstream" Zionist culture progressively weakened,[5] as evidenced in many literary, theatrical and cinematic texts.

The weakening of the secular mainstream was also caused by the concomitant strengthening of several secondary cultures, prominent among which are the various religious subcultures. That of the religious-Zionist group, whose nucleus forms an important component of the West Bank settlements, has a large and sympathetic audience among the religious and traditional middle-class *Ashkenazi* [of European origin]

---

[4] Baruch Kimmerling, "War of Cultures", *Ha'Aretz*, 7 January 1996. (Hebrew)
[5] "The Israeli is again not master of his own home", notes Gershon Shaked, by "Israeli" meaning the *Ashkenazi* Jew. Gershon Shaked, "Light, Shadow and Multiplication (the Hebrew Literature in Dialectic Struggle with a Changing Reality)", *Alpayim*, 4, 1991, 130. (Hebrew)

population. Side by side with this culture, goes that of the ultra-Orthodox sector, which for many years was alienated from the Zionist State. In the last decade, however, this alienation has undergone great change and the negative attitude has turned to one of lively political activity and a nationalist approach in matters concerning the Jewish–Arab dispute. These changes, along with others still concealed, have found theatrical expression in the last decade. The religious, for whom the theatre is "set apart", have adopted a strategy which uses the tools of the "media" of the dominant, secular section of society in order to advance their own interests.

The cultural war between the secular and the religious began in the 1870s. The *Haskala* [Jewish Enlightenment] movement set out to determine new cultural norms to replace those of Orthodox Judaism, according to which a Jew is someone who keeps the Jewish laws and whose entire lifestyle complies with all the demands of the *halacha* [the Jewish religious law]. The Jewish Enlightenment struggled to administer secular education, to involve Jews in the surrounding society through employing the language of that society, adopting its mode of attire and dealing in the economy. A change also took place in the approach to the Jewish tradition, which was now examined with the tools of rationality, which rejected such beliefs as a favoured divine providence for the Jews. The Enlightenment turned to the Bible as a source, consequently turning its back on the *halacha* literature that had evolved over a thousand years, and which was perceived as holding back the merging of the Jewish culture into the general culture. This turning to the Bible also served as a lever in renewing the Hebrew language and employing it in the creation of artistic works. Plays (unstaged) in biblical Hebrew were written during this period and I shall relate to several of them below.

An even more extreme attempt at revival and reform was carried out by the Zionist movement in the 19th century. It relinquished religion, in both practice and theory, as a unifying factor for the Jewish people and as a determining factor in the question of who is a Jew. Zionism established entirely new norms: a shared fate, a shared land, Hebrew as a shared language and, above all, shared nationalist aspirations. Israeli culture is founded upon the secularisation of Jewish traditions – a blend of the old with the new; with emphasis on the new. From the beginning of the Zionist revival Hebrew secularism drew closer to the distant biblical past and distanced itself from the nearer, Diaspora past, to the extent of openly rejecting the place from which so many of the founders of the State had come – the Jewish township. It is no coincidence that several of the early plays staged by Habima which featured a Jewish East-European township (the *shtetl*) were largely perceived by the Jewish audiences in Europe as anti-Semitic.

Gershon Shaked, describing the revolutionary changes made by Zionism to everyday language and culture, refers to the negative side activated by this ideology:

> The new Israeli culture also arose from rejection and repulsion. Its choice was not only positive. Zionism rejected the ghetto culture and was repelled by western culture. It sought new sources within the revolutionary experience: an old world pared to the essentials, and from the ruins of which would be built a new world.[6]

These were far-reaching changes in the perception of the nature and essence of the Jewish people, and it is little wonder that all the religious streams, even those coming from the Enlightenment movement, despite their differences of opinion, condemned (and some still condemn) Zionism, equating it with heresy.

A small group of orthodox Jews, Mizrahi, did make an attempt to bridge between Zionism and its nationalist ambitions and the Jewish religion, establishing the option of religious-Zionism. However, the ultra-Orthodox population organized the Agudat Israel which fought a head-on battle against this "heretical" Zionism. The Aguda were supported by the various Hassidic leaders' courts and *yeshivot* [colleges for Torah study] populated by *Mithnagdim* [objectors to Hassidism], all of which intensified the war against Zionism. This development, which began at the end of the last century, reached its peak during the First World War and continued up to the Second World War. The Holocaust, which affected all of European Jewry, turned the Zionist Land of Israel into a place of refuge also for many of the ultra-Orthodox, who founded new communities. As long as their power remained weak, the ultra-Orthodox appeared to be integrating into the *Yishuv* [the Jewish community in the pre-Statehood period] in all walks of life without relinquishing their own particular lifestyle. Following the founding of the State of Israel, Agudat Israel joined the State Council and thus began an important change in the attitude of some sectors of Orthodox Jewry to the secular State. Concomitantly large communities of the ultra-Orthodox continued to perceive the State as a direct extension of the Zionist Movement which should be forced to radical change. Others related to the State as a foreign government, from which everything possible should be taken with no obligations whatsoever in exchange. The exemption of *yeshiva* students from military service and the increased flow of State funds to the *yeshivot* reflect this approach. Developments

---

[6] Gershon Shaked, "Shall we Find Sufficient New Strength: On Behalf of Israeli Secularism", *No Other Place: On Literature and Society*, Tel Aviv, Ha'Kibbutz Ha'Meuchad, 1988, 25. (Hebrew)

also occurred in the religious-Zionist (Mizrahi) camp which gained in strength and established its own vast educational system. This took two extremes: one, the emphasis on Zionism underwent a change to emphasis on religion. The nationalist-religious party acted and still acts to establish religious laws, which are imposed upon all the country's citizens and restrict the secular: laws and statutes giving religious authority over marriage and divorce, burial and religious courts of law, and laws on the subjects of *kashrut* and the Sabbath. The religious-Zionist education also began to feature signs of an increasingly ultra-Orthodox nature. Many youngsters belonging to this movement joined anti-Zionist, ultra-Orthodox *yeshivot*. The second trend to the extreme began among religious-Zionist youth, who after the Six Day War (1967) began their campaign for a "Greater Israel", becoming a central factor in establishing the settlements in the occupied territories in the West Bank. In addition to the above, traditional and religious oriental Jews began to organize their own political party and movement – "Shas", which in fact rebelled against the *Ashkenazi* ultra-Orthodox establishment, setting up an oriental (*Sephardi*) alternative. Although these parties and movements constitute only about one fifth of the Israeli parliament, their political power is far greater.

When one examines the Jewish Israeli population's views about matters of faith, religion and a fundamental world vision,[7] a picture of a traditional to religious society appears; however, one that is also Zionist and of mixed orientation: secular, religious-secular and religious. Thus, for example, a sample survey of the population in 1993 defined itself as 2% non-Zionist ultra-Orthodox; 3% Zionist ultra-Orthodox; 9% religious-Zionist; 36% traditional (a vague category, mainly of oriental Jews and native-born Israelis, incorporating those who fulfil some of the religious commandments but do not live a full religious life); 4% Conservative or Reform; and 45% secular who do not belong to any religious stream. Despite this, however, 90% of the Jewish population in Israel define themselves as Zionists, and 94% are proud of their Jewish identity.

A particularly interesting wide and permanent division exists between "total believers" and those who do not believe at all. Both extremes possess a hard-core ideological nucleus: about 16% who believe in religion, uphold the religious commandments and possess a religious view of the world; and about 15% who could be defined as "total secularists" in their beliefs. There is considerable overlap between the non-believers and those who make up the theatre audiences, for

---

[7] Shlomit Levy, Hanna Levinsohn and Elihu Katz, *Beliefs, Observances and Social Relations among Israeli Jews*, Jerusalem, Guttman Institute of Applied Social Research, Jerusalem, 1993. (Hebrew)

whom theatre is a unique gathering place: "a secular synagogue". Between these two groups falls the majority, which practices selectivity, reflecting various degrees of faith and fulfilment of the religious commandments.

The discussion of theatrical texts in their social and ideological context, which constitutes the main theme of this book, is only just beginning. I have therefore borrowed tools and concepts from literary theory and cultural and theatrical sociology and adapted them for my study. In this Introduction I present some of the components of this method, which still remains to be fully consolidated.

Repertoire. The study of a theme within the repertoire of a national theatre, particularly in connection with Israeli society, requires the examination of its social and political context and of the ideologies at the "base of [Pavis's] iceberg". The ideological component plays a central role in the repertoire of the Hebrew theatre. It influences the majority of the plays written, as well as those translated from other languages and adapted to fit the goals that advance the needs of an embryonic society. This is an ideology that "writes" itself by means of playwrights who are frequently unaware of the fact that they are activated by the Zionist discourse.[8] Nonetheless, in the last decade the Israeli playwright has put on stage the difficulties of a divided society and the need for critical examination of the ideology which created the Hebrew State. These issues, which Nurith Gertz relates to writers and film makers, are equally relevant to theatre practitioners:

> [that] obliged Israeli society to examine its Zionist narratives, its internal contradictions – those between itself and reality and between itself and the Utopian pretensions of Zionism as a nationalist doctrine based upon a universal humanist morality.[9]

When, for example, an Israeli playwright wishes to escape from reality by dreaming of a solution to the conflict he is dealing with, his critical stand swiftly brings him back to the fact that there is no hope to be found in illusion. The strong desire for a solution to the dispute with the Arabs exemplifies the tension that exists between the desire for conciliation and the terror attacks and acts of revenge that come in their wake; a contradiction that finds its expression in dozens of "love stories" between two representatives of the two nations. Such plays express a frank desire for peace common to both the playwrights and their

---

[8] Yitzhak Laor, *Narratives with no Natives*, Tel Aviv, Ha'Kibbutz Ha'Meuchad, 1995, 115–70. (Hebrew)

[9] Nurith Gertz, *Captive of a Dream: National Myths in Israeli Culture*, Tel Aviv, Am Oved, 1995, 11–2. (Hebrew)

audiences; but the daily conflicts and fear of the "Other" force upon all these plays an ending that tends to the pessimistic and frustrates any chance of the hoped for solution.

Most of the plays to which we shall refer serve as an argument for "public thought" which, according to Yossef Gorny, is: "a pronounced cultural phenomenon, publicistic and pluralistic, which attempts to explain reality and to direct its process according to historical tradition, moral principles and also religious belief."[10] Gorny considers journalism to be the main tool of "public thought", but he also includes literature. Theatre is an important stage for Israeli public thought. A study of theatre in its social aspects, particularly from the perspective of "public thought", can be helped by Pierre Bourdieu's encompassing concept of "field". The term "field" (*champ*) can be characterized as a collection of factors and strategies linked by a common denominator – such as the field of economics, politics, religion or theatre. A field is fashioned and influenced by other fields including all their negative and positive factors. In theatre, the constant competition between mainstream and experimental ("alternative") theatre shapes both competitors. Bourdieu also includes within "field" any institution which touches upon the field: theatre itself, the government or local authority which subsidises it, other sponsors, the critics;[11] the socio-professional biographies of the theatre practitioners (*trajectoire*); the social, economic and historical circumstances behind the plays; the target audience and its social characteristics; means of manifesting the text; marketing methods, public relations and advertising.[12]

The question of a theatre's repertoire contents, i.e. what can be considered a theatrical text, is bound up with the attitude to "high" culture and "popular" or "fringe" culture. In general, Israeli theatre research tends to deal with theatre as "high" culture. This approach usually includes the plays staged by the public theatres (Habima, The Cameri, Haifa Municipal, Beer Sheba Municipal, The Jerusalem Khan and Bet Lessin theatres), but does not touch upon the "fringe" plays – fringe theatre, stand-up comedy, commercial theatre, musicals, entertainment shows, community theatre, educational theatre, *purimspiel* and appearances by religious preachers as performers. In recent years there has been a move, albeit as yet insignificant, from discussion of the "professional" theatre towards an examination of non-canonical and non-mainstream plays. The most prominent example of this is *Arbeit Macht Frei in Toitland*

---

[10] Yossef Gorny, *The Quest for a Collective Identity*, Tel Aviv, Am Oved, 1990, 14–15. (Hebrew)
[11] Pierre Bourdieu, *La Distinction: Critique sociale du jugement*, Paris, Les Éditions de Minuit, 1979, 260–66.
[12] Pierre Bourdieu, *Les Règles de l'art*, Paris, Seuil, 201–45; 249–92.

Europa, staged by the Theatre Centre of Akko (1991). This was a highly exceptional show on the fringes of theatre which "forced" itself onto the theatrical field.[13] From the ideological aspect "fringe" theatrical texts are particularly important for the fact that the "Other", like the religious figure, must present his own perspective mainly from the fringes, being unable to penetrate the repertoire of the public theatres.

The Israeli cultural system, especially highbrow culture – the fine arts, music, dance and literature – is a system whose ideological and political concepts match. The majority of both artistic creators and audience belong to a liberal social group with similar opinions. This is equally true for most of Hebrew literature, which was a "step-sister" art to Hebrew theatre, and which continues to contribute texts for adaptation to the theatre. There is a similar affinity with cinema, dance, the fine arts and music. In order to pinpoint theatre within the general cultural field of writers, artists, musicians and film-makers, we shall complete the picture by comparing issues that arise from the various plays with other artistic creations which present the Jewishness of Israelis.

Examining the *intertextual* links between plays and works from the other arts enables one to determine the things in common among a large body of artistic works. Such a repertoire served at first to consolidate a new national identity, and later on to reveal its conflicts and contradictions.

John Fiske differentiates between "horizontal" and "vertical" intertextuality.[14] Horizontal intertextuality refers to ways of organisation such as themes and genres, both of which can assist a "reading" of the Israeli theatre repertoire. Israeli society is "multi-conflictual",[15] as reflected in several of the central themes of its theatre repertoire: the Jewish–Arab dispute, the increasing conflicts between secular and religious Jews, and the rift between the different ethnic communities. The genre provides a strategy to introduce critical viewpoints. By staging the conflict between the religious and the secular in Israel, which I characterise as "self-hatred", playwrights and other theatre practitioners chose at first to present the rift through "the back door" of satire, then by means of "documentary" theatre, and only in the 1990s did they begin to employ realistic presentational means in melodrama, realistic plays or television drama. Moreover, the choice of genre was generally suited to the ideological statement or to avoiding it.[16] Such choice is also made according

---

[13] Dan Urian, "Arbeit macht Frei in Toitland Europa", *Theatre Forum*, 3, Spring 1993, 60–66.

[14] John Fiske, *Television Culture*, London and New York, Routledge 1987, 108–27.

[15] Dan Horowitz, Moshe Lissak, *Trouble in Utopia: The Overburdened Polity of Israel*, Tel Aviv, Am Oved 1990, 69. (Hebrew)

[16] Dominique Maingueneau, *Le Contexte de l'oeuvre littéraire: énonciation, écrivain, société*, Paris, Dunod, 1993, 68–71.

to the genre's status within the theatrical hierarchy. For example, the choice of female actresses in stand-up comedy is the consequence of the lowly status of women's theatre and stand-up comedy in the Israeli theatrical field. Intertextual relationships also exist between the semiotic components of theatre. Playwrights attire their "Other" characters (Arabs, religious Jews, oriental Jews) in *keffiyot* [Arab headgear], long black coats and oriental garb, respectively; Arab music, *hazzanut* [prayer accompanied by song and melody] or oriental music accompany the actions of these figures; other semiotic characterising features such scenery, gestures, pronunciation and accessories repeatedly "float" from play to play, assisting the spectator's identification of the "Other" according to the ready-made stereotypic example. Occasionally, they (sometimes unconsciously) reinforce the stereotype and sometimes they try to indicate its failings as a crass generality.

A study of the theatre repertoire in connection with a particular thematics requires the use of quantitative and qualitative methods. Quantitatively, the "Jewish subject" has been located on the fringes of Israeli theatre, almost dismissed.[17] However, in recent years, with the heightening of the secular-religious conflict, it has begun to become an important issue. The qualitative aspect examines the unique nature of those plays which I term "key productions" and their theatrical means of expression. These productions are of particular importance in relation to issues of public controversy. Such productions make their appearance during periods when the conflict they present is about to face a change, a crossroads or a climax. One interesting example is *The Jerusalem Syndrome* by Yehoshua Sobol that was staged by the Haifa Municipal Theatre (1987) several days before the outbreak of the *intifada* [Palestinian uprising]. Sobol had not foreseen the uprising, which broke out during the rehearsal period, but he was able to imagine the possibility of a similar reality: "While writing *The Jerusalem Syndrome* I experienced the country being swept away in images of dread and hatred [...] addicted to its fears and awash in violent and destructive urges."[18] These "key productions" are generally the result of a long process of "public debate" outside the theatre. Inside the theatre they are aided by indirect strategies that pave the way to changing the accepted norms they are about to break. The play *The Palestinian Girl*, also by Sobol, staged by the Haifa Municipal Theatre (1985), was one of the first expressions, following the war in Lebanon, of recognition of the Palestinian existence. One of its innovations lay in its giving title (normally forbidden or repressed) to the

---

[17] Approximately 100 plays among a repertoire of thousands. From a study of mainstream public theatres and fringe theatres. In comparison, the Jewish–Arab problem has been staged hundreds of times.

[18] Dan Urian, "The Ostrich Syndrome", *Chetz*, 1, April 1989, 96. (Hebrew)

"Other". The indirect strategy that "softened" the radical approach of the play was to use the distancing means of a play-within-a-play – the filming of a television film within the play. The reception of such plays, and the ensuing public debate,[19] generally become events which attract much attention. Such a "key production" thereby creates a turnaround in context, and in the theatrical presentation of the debate,[20] as well as in the subsequent public discussion. Gershon Shaked's reference to the relationship between literary works and society is equally valid for such "key" productions:

> The materials available to the writers are derived from their social surroundings and conditioned by it. The literary work in turn reaffects the reality from which it has taken its materials, from the social models already moulded as perspectives and points of departure. The literary work organizes the materials in order to illustrate them, and the norms they reflect, from a new perspective. Reality as a model returns to become a new model of reality, leading us to return and examine our world from another perspective.[21]

The following plays in particular dealt with the secular-religious schism: *Status Quo Vadis* by Yehoshua Sobol (1973); *Kiddush* by Shmuel Hasfari (1986, 1995); *Fleischer* by Yigal Even-Or (1993). As we shall see, they played an important role in the debate on secular-religious relations in Israel and "produced" many additional texts in the media and on the public and political stages.

The Israeli theatre repertoire includes several Jewish components:

(a) Jewish authors who did not write in Hebrew, such as Shalom Aleichem (Shalom Rabinowitz), I.L. Peretz, Shalom Asch, Isaac Bashevis-Singer and Bernard Malamud, are perceived as documenting the *shtetl* [Jewish township in Eastern Europe] of the past and the Jewish Diaspora of the present. Their plays and stage adaptations of their short stories and novels have been presented in the past in versions generally tending toward the comic or the melodramatic. From the 1980s on, the style of dramatic presentation of Jewish communities, subjects and places underwent change, and began to be seen in a serious light. Several of these plays were highly successful, possibly due to nostalgic longings and the search for identity.

(b) The novels and stories of S.Y. Agnon constitute an important component. They have been adapted for the theatre by several directors,

---

[19] Fiske, note 14, terms this type of reception "vertical intertextuality" and includes within it the "secondary" texts of the press and public debates and the "tertiary" texts of spectator reactions and discussions, and correspondence published or sent to the play's creators.

[20] Yona Hadari-Ramage, *Thinking It Over, Conflicts in Israeli Public Thought*, Yad Tabenkin, Ramat Efal and Yediot Aharonot, 1994, 638. (Hebrew)

[21] Gershon Shaked, note 6, 8. (Hebrew)

in particular Yossi Yzraely, Yoram Falk and Yaakov Raz. Agnon is a religious writer who gained success (and a Nobel prize for literature in 1966) mainly among secular readers as a sort of mediator between the two different cultural worlds. Notwithstanding, the majority of plays adapted from Agnon were not favourably received by their audiences, possibly due to the difficulties imposed by Agnon's particular use of language and the religious cultural link.

(c) In the 1970s and 1980s three secular Israeli artists – Yossi Yzraely, Danny Horowitz and Yaakov Raz – attempted a new way, albeit marginal from the point of view of its effect and the size of its audiences, of dealing theatrically with Jewish sources and texts from the Talmud, the *Kabbalah* and Hassidism. All these artists chose "experimental" staging for their productions, revealing the difficulty that a secular artist encounters with materials from the religious-Jewish traditions.

(d) Several of the plays from the 1980s and 1990s pointedly raise the question of the relationship between Zionism and Judaism. Yehoshua Sobol in particular dealt with this issue for the first time on stage in *Soul of a Jew* at the Haifa Municipal Theatre (1982). The play's central theme is that of the suicide of Otto Weininger (1880–1903), a Viennese Jewish philosopher who converted in the wake of his hatred of his own Jewishness. Weininger himself related to Zionism in his book *Geschlecht und Charakter* (1903), perceiving it as anti-Jewish or as negating Judaism. Sobol chose Weininger partially for the tense Judaism–Zionism connection, but even more so, he says, because of the War in Lebanon which formed the background to the play:

> [Weininger's] work *Geschlecht und Charakter* expresses to a certain extent his admiration for Zionism. He claimed that Zionism represents everything noble that remains of the Jewish soul, but which has no chance, for Judaism will gnaw away at it from the inside and swallow it. Weininger means 'noble' in the German sense of valour, power and aggression. Sharon[22] is in effect the manifestation of Weininger's dream, a powerful Jew, a figure who takes no account of *goyim* [non-Jews]; quite the opposite, he strikes at them. What is powerful, military and "masculine" in the Israeli mentality in fact comprises an expression of the negative aspect of Jewish existence in the Diaspora according to Weininger's own negation of it [...] The War in Lebanon constituted the climax of this line of thought. This was not a defensive war but a masculine one – a smashing through, conquering and over-running of the area. An instigated war.[23]

---

[22] Arik Sharon was the Defence Minister during the War in Lebanon. At his initiative the planned limited campaign developed into an all out and complicated war.

[23] Shira Stav, "An Israeli Playwright and the 'Jewish Soul': an Interview with Yehoshua Sobol", *Bamah*, 134, 1993, 42. (Hebrew)

In the study of theatrical productions in their social context, I have emphasized three components that play an important role: *intentions, sociosemiotic textual analysis* and *reception*. It should be noted that it is occasionally difficult to discriminate between original intention and intention upon hindsight, and that textual analysis is affected by accompanying texts that attest to the creators' intentions (such as interviews, introductions and previous plays) and by information on their reception. In studying plays I have adopted the approach of Richard Schechner, according to which there is no single individual item of a production which does not belong or have some effect upon the whole – beginning from the preparations and ending with the spectators recollections. Schechner refers in particular to all the events that occur between actors and audience from the moment the first spectator enters the auditorium and until the departure of the very last spectator. Schechner thereby broadens the concept of theatrical text,[24] bringing it closer to a discussion in its social and ideological context.

Intentions refers to the socio-political and collective biographical background of the all those involved in creating and performing the text. The Israeli playwright, according to Lucien Goldmann's concept, is a *transindividuel*, representing the beliefs and opinions of a particular Israeli social group. His (and his group's) *vision du monde* [world view] are the "prism"[25] that mediate between social reality and its theatrical text. Just as it is possible to learn from Dickens's novels about solutions to the problems of poverty in Victorian England as provided by certain enlightened members of the British bourgeoisie in the 19th century, so too can Israeli playtexts inform us about the double-edged approach of a secular and hegemonic social group towards the various religious groups and to the Jewish tradition. Moreover, the playwright not only has the role of "public emissary", but also that of an intellectual who evaluates and criticizes his own group and is able to reveal by theatrical means the motives and interests behind its collective norms and its attitude to the groups of "Others".

Text. The majority of playwrights refer to the issue in texts dealing with the religious conflict in contemporary time. Of all the various narrative arts, theatre is the swiftest to react. A novel takes a long time to be written, and a film in Israel is a complex and difficult economic adventure. A fringe theatre play, however, based upon a rough text and

---

[24] Richard Schechner, *Performance Theory*, London, Routledge, 1988, 39.
[25] Alain Viala refers to what he terms "prismatic effects" in relation to those components which both reflect social reality and distort it, and which are created by codes and institutions and "fields" that "mediate" between society and the text. Alain Viala, "Prismatic Effects", trans. Paula Wissing, in: *Literature and Social Practice*, Philippe Desan, Priscilla Parkhurst Ferguson and Wendy Griswold, eds., Chicago and London, The University of Chicago Press, 1989, 256.

slim budget, can react swiftly to immediate events. Occasionally, due to the desire to respond extremely quickly (triggered by the great intensity of Israeli daily life) certain plays are mounted that tend to the crude, the demonstrative and, therefore, also to the stereotypic. Many Israeli theatre texts would appear to have difficulty fitting into the multi-layered image of Pavis's iceberg. Many of them openly disclose their ideological side while others only barely succeed in hiding it. It is possible that the reality forces Israeli theatre practitioners into creating unpolished statements, crude and direct. In such cases the "base of the iceberg" (social context and ideology) becomes the main part of the text. Such plays nonetheless have documentary importance, representing the desires and fears of an important group in Israeli society. It is thus not surprising that sociologists use these texts as evidence for their claims: Moshe Lissak, for example, in referring to social-military relations, supports his arguments with three plays which demonstrate the critical attitude to the Israeli army. All three were staged by non-mainstream theatres: *Queen of Bathtub* by Hanoch Levin (1970), *The Governor of Jericho* by Yossef Mundi (1975) and *Ephraim Returns to the Army* by Yitzhak Laor (1989).[26] These plays were given fewer than twenty performances, before small audiences. Their effect, however, both during the time of performance and for the following twenty years, was far greater. They were discussed by the media, the High Court, the Knesset [Israeli parliament] and in academic and political circles. Most of the plays with which we shall deal constitute similar expressions of the desire of their creators to determine a standpoint and attempt to make their influence felt, and sometimes they even succeed in doing so.

In studying and comparing these texts, I have used theatre *sociosemiotics*. I base my approach upon Maria Shevtsova who claims that: "Fiction is indeed fiction but is nevertheless built out of social signs."[27] In "reading" theatrical productions it is important to discern the semiotic aspect, for it is this which directs us towards a system of signs such as word and tone, gesture, movement, costume, place, scenery, music, accessories. These sign systems assisted the playwrights, directors, actors and designers to stage their own particular concept of the controversial issues, whether directly or indirectly (for example by means of music or scenery).

Sociosemiotics can be illustrated by Moshe Lissak's reference to TZAHAL [the Israeli Armed Forces]. Lissak claims that this is an army which cannot be coerced into any "rigid and harsh discipline in any area whatsoever. For this reason TZAHAL is the most unkempt army in the

---

[26] Hadari-Ramage, note 20, 339.
[27] Maria Shevtsova, "The Sociology of the Theatre, Part Three: Performance", *New Theatre Quarterly*, 19, August 1989, 292.

world."[28] Indeed, all three of the plays referred to by Lissak, as a sociologist studying the relationship of Israeli society with its armed forces, present images of slovenly dressed soldiers on stage, as do dozens of similar plays. Other examples of the use of clothing can be found in plays featuring the ultra-Orthodox. These figures are always garbed in black, just as in the extratheatrical reality, while the secular figures in these plays are usually attired in light coloured clothing. This contrast in colours emphasizes the (secular) audience's conflict between their self-image as "sons of light" and the religious "sons of darkness". Objects too may become loaded with ideological significance – in several of the plays in the 1990s a stage property knife represented the violent side of Palestinian society and an intensification of the threatening Arab image in the wake of the *intifada*. Celebrity actors also function as symbols in the semiotic web of the play. Tendentious casting of Arab actors in translated plays anchors such plays within the local context and the dispute with the Palestinians. The Arab actor Yossef Abu Warda was cast as a black character in Athol Fugard's play *The Blood Knot* at the Beer Sheba Municipal Theatre (1978). Makram Khouri, also an Arab actor, played the role of Lopakhin in Chekhov's *The Cherry Orchard* directed by Omri Nizan at Habima theatre (1988), representing the fears of a Jewish-Israeli society of immigrants that the peasant's son dispossessed of his lands would return to retake them.

An analysis of theatrical texts from their social and ideological aspect incorporates the historio-political and social background that enabled the matching of the signs to their references. In order to describe the circumstances of the staging of these plays I have made use of research by historians, sociologists and psychologists who have studied Israeli society. These studies help to map the reality to which the various theatre practitioners relate. The findings also help to explain the textual presence or absence of the "Other" during any particular period. They likewise assist in determining the similarity or dissimilarity in the traits of the religious Jew depicted in the theatre, compared to how he is perceived among the secular and traditionally observant communities in the extratheatrical social reality.

Reception. The secular-religious theme provides a clear example of the active involvement of Israeli theatre in the external reality and in the process of change being undergone by the collective self-image of an important group in Israeli society. Moreover, Israeli theatre is perceived by its audiences as a "high" cultural activity, whose contents are considered to be of importance and which takes place in specifically designated locations whose titles are indicative of their nature, such as "Palace of the

---

[28] Hadari-Ramage, note 20, 339.

Theatre". The majority of spectators are relatively well educated adults, secular or traditional, and of western origin.[29] Frequently, therefore, as part of a social ritual, these spectators choose original plays for their "subject matter", in order to "feel themselves part of Israeli society."[30] This would appear to be the reason for theatres tending to stage original Israeli plays, which nowadays comprise over half the repertoire.[31] The increasing tension between the secular and religious communities has also led to the Jewish theme making more frequent appearances in the theatre in recent years.

One important aspect of the theatre's approach to "public thought" is that of "the public nature of drama", as Georg Lukács terms the circumstances of staging a play, and its means of reception by the audience, which is carried out in a public place similar to any other type of political performances.[32] An additional component necessary for our understanding of the influence of theatre on extratheatrical reality is the number of addressees: the problem, dilemma or political argument is presented before an audience whose numbers, even for a mediocre performance, can reach tens of thousands.[33] To this, we can add what Fiske includes in "vertical intertextuality"[34]: all those same articles and other information which accompany the play and are served up by the press and electronic media, etc. Any play impugning the contents and symbols of the social status quo invites either public or political debate and, most importantly, a television coverage which lends a far greater and more widespread effect than that actually experienced by the spectators in the theatre. Consequently, plays taking a stand regarding a conflict so central

---

[29] Elihu Katz, Michael Gurevitch, *et al.*, *Leisure Culture in Israel: Types of Recreation and Cultural Needs*, Tel Aviv, Am Oved, 1973, 92, 98. Hadassah Hass *et al.*, "4. Cultural Needs", "2. Types of Cultural Needs in 1990", in: Hadassah Hass, Elihu Katz, Miriam Schiff, Shai Inbar, *Leisure Culture in Israel, Changes in Types of Cultural Activity 1970–1990*, Jerusalem, Guttman Institute for Applied Social Research, 1992, 10–17. (Hebrew)

[30] *ibid*, 1992, 16.

[31] Shosh Weitz, *Summary of Activities by Public Institutions for Culture and Arts in Israel, 1993*, Tel Aviv, Administration for Culture and Art, the Council for Culture and Art, 1994, 35. (Hebrew)

[32] Georg Lukács, *The Historical Novel*, trans. Hannah and Stanley Mitchell, Harmondsworth, Penguin, 1969, 150.

[33] Several of the plays dealing with the secular-religious issue have won great acclaim in recent years: *Fleischer* by Yigal Even-Or, directed by Amit Gazit (1993) reached a total audience of 56,264, the fifth largest number of spectators for the season. *Sheindele* by Ramy Danon and Amnon Levy, directed by Ramy Danon (1994) at the Cameri Theatre reached a total audience of 66,189. This was also the fifth largest number of spectators for that season, the second season of the play. In 1993 it took 10th place in number of spectators: 42,611. From: *Summary of Activities of Public Institutions for Culture and Arts in Israel* for 1993 and 1994. (Hebrew)

[34] see note 14, 117–24.

to Israeli society, may have a far greater ideological effect. The combination of all the above-mentioned components illustrates the importance of the debate being carried out on Israeli stages over such problematic issues as the religious-secular schism. These plays also provide evidence refuting those versions which lessen the gravity of the secular-religious conflict in Israel in the 1990s.

The abandoned argument over quantitative studies of reception, in particular the harsh criticism of Jean Duvignaud[35] in regard to such research as a meaningless accumulation of data, may indeed prove to be correct – if the relevant questionnaires have not been directed at revealing the spectator's understanding, reached as a consequence of the play he has watched. This understanding refers to aesthetic, ideological and emotional components.[36] Two of the chapters in this book have made use of questionnaires, by means of which I attempted to reach a better comprehension of the audience's "reading" of the play. The findings from these questionnaires served to support my assumptions regarding the plays' reception.

The chapters are arranged in historical and thematic order. Drama, as already noted, has, since the time of the Jewish Enlightenment, served the secular community in its conflict with the religious. Chapter One, therefore, opens with a description of the secular-religious rift, which began to occur in the last century and which has intensified towards the end of the present century. Chapter Two describes the enhanced concern of the secular community for its own Jewishness, and its expression in the theatre, especially following the 1967 War. I have chosen to exemplify this by studying one particular theatre text, *Ish Hassid Haya* by Dan Almagor (1968), one of the greatest successes ever staged by the Hebrew theatre. Chapter Three also refers to one play – *Bruria*, by the Theatre Company of Jerusalem. The play was first staged in 1982 and is still being performed today in 1998. This is a women's theatre in search of its Jewish identity, although the quest is accompanied by pointed criticism of the humiliating status of women in Judaism. Chapter Four deals with the religious "Other" – in a religious-Zionist women's theatre. It represents a new cultural phenomenon in which a group of women, with the permission of the rabbis and leaders of their communty, approach theatre as a didactic tool, primarily political, aimed at internal reinforcement of their own community and at expressing their viewpoints to the external, secular community. The final chapter returns to the

---

[35] Jean Duvignaud, *Sociologie du théâtre: Essai sur les ombres collectives*, Paris, PUF, 1965, 42–43.
[36] Marco De Marinis, "Sociologie", *Théâtre. Modes d'approche*, Bruxelles, Éditions Labor, 1987, 86–89.

beginning – to the secular-religious conflict. It studies the phenomenon of the return to Orthodox Judaism by secular individuals. Since it first made its appearance in the middle of the 1980s, this phenomenon has been accompanied by theatrical strategies on the part of the proselytizers and by harsh counter reaction by the secular theatre, manifesting the sense of threat that this trend to religious conversion elicits among the secular community.

1

"SELF-HATRED"

Since the 1980s there has been a growing number of plays in the Israeli theatre which focus on the conflict between secular and religious Jews. These theatre texts reveal the enduring nature of the negative religious stereotypes among sectors of the secular population and attest to the attitude termed by Baruch Kurzweil as "self-hatred".[1]

Most of the religious, ultra-Orthodox and nationalist-religious images that populate these plays are stereotypic in nature. Most of them also appear in the comic genres that "justify" such a depiction. The theatrical stereotype is a faithful expression of the stereotypical attitude of secular Jews to the religious, in particular to the ultra-Orthodox. Amnon Levy, a secular journalist who studied the ultra-Orthodox world, "confesses":

> Strange as it might sound, it became clear to me that the prejudices were mostly on my side, as a secular Jew, rather than on the side of the ultra-Orthodox. Suspicion, recoil and objection characterize the secular individual's relationship to the ultra-Orthodox community. A number of prejudices exist among the secular; and more than a few of them concern the ultra-Orthodox: they stink, are sexual perverts, cheats, swindlers, hypocrites, and above all primitive. Every secular individual will openly admit to having more than once heard such expressions directed against the ultra-Orthodox.[2]

These stereotypic characterizations in the theatre, and their link to extra-theatrical reality, together with an understanding of their role in the conflict, requires a few preliminary words of explanation of the relationship between the secular and the religious in Israeli society and their cultural backgrounds. Research into the secular/religious schism has tended to depict it as a relatively moderate conflict. Dan Horowitz and Moshe Lissak note that this schism, unlike the Jewish ethnic divisions or the Jewish/Arab conflict, is not dichotomous but, rather presents "levels of polarization along a one or more dimensional continuum. Between the extreme secularists and extreme religious many different shades of traditionalists can be discerned." However, "the ideological dispute over the

---

[1] Baruch Kurzweil, "On Self-Hatred in Jewish Literature", *Our New Literature – a Continuation or a Revolution?*, Jerusalem, Shoken, 1965/b, 331–401. (Hebrew)
[2] Amnon Levy, *The ultra-Orthodox*, Jerusalem, Keter, 1990, 256. (Hebrew)

question of religion has existed since the beginning of the Zionist enterprise under the shadow of the threat of a cultural rift defined in terms of
a cultural war (*Kultur Kampf*)."[3] It was the desire to avoid such a culture
war that motivated the secular public's acquiescence to the religious
community, particularly its acceptance of those laws dealing with matri-
mony and religious matters that come into conflict with the accepted
norms of the secular society, as well as in issues relating to the equality of
women, abortion, keeping the Sabbath, *kashrut*, and film and theatre censorship (an institution that was possibly particularly instrumental in
causing the theatre to raise fierce objections to the religious groups, thus
reinforcing their negative image). There have been compromises too over
freedom of research, particularly in the fields of archeology and medicine. These compromises have not always lessened the tension or the
"cultural war", in recent years in particular, due to the awakening of
Jewish religious fundamentalism, the phenomenon of secular individuals returning to Orthodoxy and the politicization of religion. The process
of "secularisation", modernisation and hedonism, signs of which can be
found in every facet of Israeli society, and which constitutes the antithesis of the religious world vision, has also had its effect.

Comprehensive contemporary research by Shlomit Levy,
Hanna Levinsohn and Elihu Katz (December 1993) has shown that "the
most negative criticism regarding religious/secular relationships takes
place among the least religious groups" which mainly comprise immigrants of western origin and their children, as well as the more highly
educated sector. The tendency of this group "is to ascribe the blame to
the religious for the lack of good relations between the secular and
religious factions [...] the secular blame the religious for lack of consider-
ation more than the religious blame the secular."[4]

The described "conflict group" shares several important characteristics with spectators at the Israeli theatre. According to research by
Hadassah Hass *et al.*, theatre-going is directly connected to level of education, ethnic origin and degree of religiosity:

> The most active [theatre] visitors are well-educated (13 or more years of
> education), traditionalist and secular native Israelis of western origin
> [...] the highest percentage of non theatre-goers are religiously obser-
> vant with a low level of education (up to 11 years), and of oriental origin
> (88%). A higher level of education among the religious is reflected in
> a moderate rise in the percentage of theatre-goers. However, even here

---

[3] Dan Horowitz, Moshe Lissak, *Trouble in Utopia: The Overburdened Polity of Israel*, Tel Aviv,
Am Oved, 1990, 69, 188. (Hebrew)

[4] Shlomit Levy, Hanna Levinsohn and Elihu Katz, *Beliefs, Observances and Social Relations
among Israeli Jews in Israel*, Jerusalem, Guttman Institute for Applied Social Research,
1993, 12. (in Hebrew)

among the more highly educated religious community (13 years or more of education) there are many who do not visit the theatre.[5]

According to these findings, together with the implications of the repertoire (which will be dealt with below), the majority of spectators at the theatre are secular Jews belonging to a group which perceives the religious (ultra-Orthodox and nationalist religious) as a rival which it must confront by repudiating its beliefs. In this almost ritual experience the recurring narrative is that of ripping off the mask and revealing the negative motives behind the religious "Other". In most of the theatre texts that serve the secular group in the conflict, therefore, religious characters are depicted as stereotypes. The importance of stereotypes in a discussion dealing with a social divide was already discerned when the term was first coined by Walter Lippmann, who explained it as a defence mechanism for a certain tradition and for viewpoints adopted by a certain group.[6] Richard Dyer, studying the social function of stereotypes in fiction (mainly cinema), notes that the stereotype in fiction and theatre is restricted *a priori* in its action within the narrative; in effect perpetuating the social definition and the borders between different social groups.[7]

The religious characters in Israeli theatre are stereotypes of a special kind: they include subject and object, the defined object and part of the identity of the definer. This differs, for example, from the Arab "Other" who, within the Hebrew culture, is perceived as a savage and threatening stranger as well as being of low social caste, humiliated and exploited. In order to deal with obstacles such as censorship and criticism, the theatre practitioners need to employ oblique strategies when presenting the religious "Other", thus enabling them to present him as a derided and repulsive character, despite their mutual national and cultural origins.

The religious stereotype possesses obvious external characteristics that have become decidedly fixed in most of the figures, particularly in recent years: black garb, hat or knitted skullcap for men, hat or head scarf for women, beard, sidelocks, mode of speech (nasal, fast); a special vocabulary that mixes different "languages" – quotes from Jewish sources, Yiddish; "Jewish" gestures. Costume, in this connection, plays a central role due to its semiotic function in extra-theatrical reality. Amnon Levy states:

> Everything *black*, is what the secular person sees when he looks at the
> ultra-Orthodox. Black clothes, from head to toe, covering a person who

[5] Hadassah Hass *et al.*, "4. The Cultural Need", "2. Types of Cultural Needs in 1990", in: Hadassah Hass, Elihu Katz, Miriam Schiff, Shai Inbar, *Leisure Culture in Israel: Changes in Types of Cultural Activity 1970–1990*, Jerusalem, Guttman Institute for Applied Social Research, Centre for Information and Research of the Public Council for Culture and Art, 1992, 10–11. (Hebrew)

[6] Walter Lippmann, *Public Opinion*, New York, Macmillan, 1956, 96.

[7] Richard Dyer, "The Role of Stereotypes", *The Matter of Images, Essays on Representations*, London and New York, Routledge, 1993, 11–18.

is different, a rival. They are all black, says the secularist, partly fearful partly stirred to anger by this incomprehensible phenomenon [...] the ideology behind the black clothes is simple: to differentiate, to preserve the Jewish ghetto.[8]

The history of the secular/religious schism from its beginnings and up until recent times reveals that the secular perception of the religious stereotype has not diminished; rather, the negative characteristics attributed to it have increased and figures from the nationalist-religious and *Sephardic* ultra-Orthodox communities have been added to it. Since *Megaleh Temirin* by Yossef Pearl (1819) and up to *Fleischer* by Yigal Even-Or (1993), the recurring pattern has been one of an almost unchanged stereotype of the religious Jew as determined by secularists. This same phenomenon, occurring in different places and throughout different periods in time, illustrates the intensity of the conflict and the extent of the schism.

The period of the Jewish enlightenment [*Haskala*], according to Nathan Rotenstreich, initiated the division "between Judaism and Jews".[9] This occurred when "the starting point for Hebrew enlightened education was a recognition of the gap between Jewish life-style as it was and between the demands of time." (p. 147) In fiction, and even biography (such as *The Life of Salomon Maimon* 1792/3), the enlightened portray a religious stereotype of failure and repulsion. In particular they deal with the Hassid and the *Zaddik* [Hassidic leader]. Hassidism attracted this attention due to its nature as a very successful popular movement and the period of its development coinciding with that of Jewish enlightenment. The competition and conflict between the two movements was unavoidable and expressed in unconventional and harsh terms. The satires of Yossef Pearl (1773–1839) were particularly well known, directed mainly against the Hassidim. The world of the Hassidim is depicted by the enlightenment as full of intrigue, to be revealed by the ingenious devices of satire. They attempted to fragment this world from within through fictional confessions by the *Zaddik*, or fake correspondence that derided the Hassidic leaders and their values. Satire tried to devalue the meaning of Hassidic tales, the "wonders" performed by the *Zaddik* were presented as deliberately faked, and the Hassidic language was mocked.

In Zionism from its outset, the negative stereotype of the Orthodox Diaspora Jew was a prevalent common figure; Eliezer Don-Yehiya described this stereotype thus:

> Passive and dependent, "over-spiritual", occupied in "non-productive" jobs, dishonest in social relations, selfish, unfeeling, rude and uncouth,

---

[8] Amnon Levy, note 2, 31.
[9] Natan Rotenstreich, *Jewish Thought in the New Era*, Tel Aviv, Am Oved, 1966, 17. (Hebrew)

detached, cut-off from nature and art, closed, weak, feeble, fearful, lacking self-respect, over-pedantic, conservative and stubborn […].[10]

Theodor Herzl, visionary of the Jewish State, and also a playwright, presented such a stereotyped figure in *The New Ghetto*.[11] This play was staged in Vienna in 1898 at the Karltheater, and the censor who had originally had reservations regarding the content, restricted himself to banning the unsympathetic rabbi in the play from appearing onstage. The "rabbiner", Dr Friedheimer, "plays the stock exchange" (p. 176), and according to the stage directions he behaves "in a slightly Hassidic fashion" (*ibid*); the rabbiner sees anti-Semitism as a blessing: "It has its good side too. Since the outbreak of anti-Semitism in the land I see more fear of heaven. Anti-Semitism is a warning to us, to remain faithful to our unity, that we may not abandon the God of our forefathers, as many did." (*ibid*).

Presenting the negative and disclaiming the religious life-style, is found in particular in the new Hebrew literature. A noted commentator, Baruch Kurzweil, also indicated its results among Israeli youth, who require the ritual of exorcising the demons in their confrontation with religious tradition and its representatives. Several such rituals, as we shall see, took place in the theatre:

> This Judaism of previous generations appears strange to a great part of Israeli youth. The educational material of the present generation does not only not have the ability to uproot this sense of alienation, but even increases it […] it creates a sort of demonic attitude. You can't live with demons […] this is really the situation in many cases. It creates hostile effects, because the change is so close and even requires identification between the hating subject and the hated object.[12]

In the Hebrew theatre, which from the outset identified itself with the nationalist Zionist rebirth, that was turned towards the future and thus negated the Diaspora past, signs of this negative, religious, ghetto-like Jew can be found. A debate on the issue accompanied the play *The Dybbuk* by S. Anski and continued with *The Treasure* by Shalom

---

[10] Eliezer Don-Yehieh, "Secularization, Negation and Combination of Approaches to Traditional Judaism and its Concepts in Socialist-Zionism", *Kivunim* 8, 1980, 32. See also: Yoachim Doron, "Classical Zionism and Modern anti-Semitism – Parallels and Influences (1883–1914)", *Ha'Zionut*, 8, 1983, 57–101. (Hebrew)

[11] Theodor Herzl, "The New Ghetto", *Hechal Bourbon*, trans. into Hebrew: M. Z. Wolfpovsky, Tel Aviv, M. Newman, 1961, 159–216.

[12] Baruch Kurzweil, "The Significance and Origins of the 'Young Hebrews' Movement (*Canaanim*)", *Our New Literature – Continuation or Revolution?*, Jerusalem and Tel Aviv, Shoken, 1959, 285–93. (Hebrew)

Aleichem. When these plays were mounted by Habima during its second tour of Europe (1929–1931), there were Jews in Europe who saw *The Treasure* as a truly anti-Semitic play. When Habima performed it in Warsaw, the critic Y. M. Neiman of the Yiddish journal *Heint* stated that Habima had totally destroyed the way of life of the *shtetl* [Jewish township in Central and Eastern Europe prior to the Second World War] in order to build a new life and new society: "What do you want from these *shtetl* Jews? Leave them alone in their mistaken dreams [...] Why is Habima's anger so great? Why does it so sadistically slash the living flesh of these people?"[13] An Israeli critic also wrote: "While I was sitting in the theatre, I heard someone in the audience whisper a comment: it's a bit anti-Semitic... and it is possible that this person was partially right. For there is a slight element of 'anti-Semitism' in every Israeli work that does not come to terms [...] with the Jewish degeneration."[14] One of the climaxes in *The Dybbuk*, was a dance by the townspeople: a scene overflowing with such loathsome details as a woman picking lice from her daughter's head.

The "Tartuffe" Stereotype

The religious stereotype in Hebrew theatre is an instrumental one, functioning above all to emphasize its own alienness and to uncover its falsity. The dramatic narrative in which such characters appear aims at uncovering what is hidden beneath the mask of those who complicate the lives of others, and at revealing their human weaknesses. The sexual instinct plays an important role in this connection. Similar to the "blocking" character in comedy, who covets for him/herself one of the young lovers and hinders the natural course of events, so too is the religious figure presented as someone unable to resist sexual temptation, thereby becoming a stumbling block for the religious ideal. This failure to withstand temptation reveals the religious individual as no better than anyone else; it presents the prohibitions that he decrees for himself and others as being totally inconsistent with a normal way of life. The text is a means of venting frustration, for this same "Other" is constantly employing various political means in an attempt to force his own beliefs and customs upon the spectators. Such stereotypes therefore generally incorporate such traits as dishonesty and low social status, and are contrasted with the secular approach to life. A confrontation is thus created in a public and "holy" arena (the theatre is the Israeli secular "synagogue") against those with a high level of self-conviction, particularly over a possibility

---

[13] *Heint*, 4 March 1930.
[14] *Ha'Aretz*, 2 December 1928. (Hebrew)

that worries many secularists – the return to ultra-Orthodoxy (as we shall see in Chapter 5). Ironically, the most famous of all those who "returned to the ultra-Orthodox fold" – Uri Zohar, uses his cinematic acting, editing and directing experience to produce video-cassettes of religious tracts that are theatrical in both composition and content, and which he uses to present the "emptiness" and "worthlessness" of secular values and customs.

More than any other play from the classic repertoire, Molière's *Tartuffe* has attracted numerous adaptations and translations for the Hebrew (and Yiddish) stage. This is Molière's most successful play, in no small part due to the many ideological purposes that it can serve. In the last three centuries *Tartuffe* has served the "forces of light" in the French theatre in their struggle against the "forces of religious reactionaries". Hebrew drama has made use of several of the play's motifs, particularly that of *l'Imposteur* [the hypocrite]. Israeli theatre has chosen to assail the religious extremists, to show the lustful nature concealed beneath their masks, and thus disclose the real character of the ultra-Orthodox community. The strategy of "borrowing" a text from the world repertoire, like that of adapting a comedy to satire,[15] aids the secular playwright or adaptor in harshly criticising the religious under the guise of the "classics" or satire, or both.

From the historical point of view, translations and adaptations of *Tartuffe* into Hebrew have appeared in print and onstage during periods when the secular/religious conflict has intensified. Since the period of the Jewish enlightenment onward the figure of Tartuffe has served the secularists in their struggle against the religious. This motif appeared, for example, in the character of the hypocrite in Adam Hacohen Lebensohn's play *Truth and Faith* (1862). Lebensohn depicted the hypocrite as someone who "presents himself to the people as 'holier than thou' with his vanities and deceptions […] like the false prophets who were told: 'Neither shall they wear a rough garment to deceive' (*Zacharia* 13:4) and who created an uproar in every generation and every nation".[16] Several of the hypocrite's characteristics bring him close to the Hassidic world which, as we have seen, drew particular condemnation from enlightened Jewry. Similar to his ecstatic mode of prayer – "to sway and bow down in prayer until my back and my flesh are exhausted in sweat" (p. 34) – so too is Rabbi Josephche in Aharon Halle-Wolfsohn's play *Rabbi Chanoch and Rabbi Josephche* (1794) called a "Jewish Tartuffe" by a German newspaper.[17] As in other "Tartuffian" plays written in Hebrew, including

---

[15] Denis Diderot, "Paradoxe sur le comédien", *Oeuvres Choisies*, Vol. 2, Paris, Larousse, 1939, 60.

[16] Lebensohn Adam Hacohen, *Truth and Faith*, Vilna, 1867, 237–8. (Hebrew)

[17] Dan Miron, "On Aharon Wolfsohn and his play *Frivolity and Hypocrisy*", Aharon Halle-Wolfsohn, *Frivolity and Hypocrisy (Rabbi Chanoch and Rabbi Josephche)*, Tel Aviv, Sifrei Siman Kriah, 1977, 29. (Hebrew)

those that appeared on the Hebrew stage, Wolfsohn introduces several characters who become permanent partners in the theatrical depiction of the schism. Three of these are vital to the secular narrative: the figure of the hypocrite whose mask is removed; the naive figure, innocently following the apparently religious lure proffered by the hypocrite; and the enlightened figure, who is occasionally also the *raisonneur* [man of reason] in the play. The rest of the *dramatis personae* represent different viewpoints in the social schism: the majority suffer from the religious coercion forced upon them by the hypocrite, as well as from the bribes and favours that he requires from them. Some figures, usually only a few, are grotesque and totally blind like Orgon's mother, Madame Pernelle, having absolute faith in the hypocrite. Sometimes simply revealing his malice is enough to banish him from the comic world and occasionally it is necessary to enlist the help, as in Molière's comedy, of a superior civil authority who represents justice. Tartuffe is the "blocking character", as termed by Northrop Frye,[18] the most threatening figure in the comic heritage – he is not a bothersome old man, an impostor, a miser or pursuing a title, but a sly rogue who enlists the religious establishment, its doctrine and, mainly, the unquestionable authority of God's emissaries, who speak in the name of the divine presence. The unravelling of the Tartuffian plot, therefore, in its different versions, involves the difficult but necessary act of returning the social order to its rightful place. Such correction of affairs cannot be restricted merely to removing the blocking character (as in Molière's other plays, in which the miser remains with his money, the impostor with his degree in medicine, or the pretentious figure with his delusions of grandeur), but ends in the religious hypocrite's complete banishment from society and his imprisonment.

The religious hypocrite appears in many such plays as a frightening and threatening, almost demonic figure, often enhanced by his black garb. To vanquish Tartuffe he must first be unmasked, which in the theatre means removing his costume while he is embroiled in planning some evil deed. His inability to control his desires reveals – literally and metaphorically – his moral nakedness and strips away his mask. The religious man, as the secular playwright reminds us, is also a man, as Molière's Tartuffe attests to himself: "Ah! pour être dévot, je n'en suis pas moins homme." [I am a religious man, but I am no less a man for that] (*Tartuffe* 3,3).

Molière's characters become "Jewishized" in Hebrew versions of *Tartuffe*. The playwrights tend towards satire. They provide familiar signs indicating a particular image, well-known to the Jewish public, which to the secularists represents the degenerative and hypocritical side

---

[18] Northrop Frye, *Anatomy of Criticism*, Princeton, New Jersey, Princeton University Press, 1971, 163–86.

of religion. Daliah Kaufman suggests that in the play *Naval the Zaddik or the Hypocrite* – a plagiarised version of *Tartuffe* – written by David Veksler (1834), the character of Tartuffe is in fact that of a well-known Hassidic figure.[19] In 1985, Yehoshua Sobol noted as the source of inspiration for his translation several familiar politician-rabbis.

The character of Orgon interests adaptors and translators no less than that of Tartuffe, for Orgon's naive insanity is what attracts the religious hypocrite to gain control over his family. In regard to the secular/religious schism, the Jewish Orgon represents the apathetic secularist or the "traditionalist" whose folly and blindness, according to this approach, enable the "righteous" figures – the rabbis, the religious politicians and the various scoundrels and liars – to take control over Jewish society.

Tartuffe serves Israeli theatre in the *Kultur Kampf* struggle of the secularists against the religious, and its production is affected by contemporary political events and conflicts. However, the identifying signs always maintain the French origin of the play.[20] The play's approach to the schism is recognisable in the dialogue, which has a strong tendency toward many "Jewish" expressions of religiosity. According to Chaim Hefer, a "reading" of such plays needs to be contextual and their interpretation should be linked to those extra-theatrical events upon which they are based, in the struggle against religious coercion.[21]

Yehoshua Sobol's translation was directed by Gedalia Besser at the Haifa Municipal Theatre in 1985, and was entirely aimed against the religious, particularly those who had returned to the ultra-Orthodox fold. Sobol's *Tartuffe* was a "protest play" against "those with pretensions of being the Holy One's representatives on earth", who are represented by Tartuffe, and against their followers as represented by Orgon: "Orgon, whose passion for Tartuffe returns him to the religious fold and turns him insane."[22]

---

[19] The *Zaddik* Avraham Yaakov Friedman (1819–1883) whose "court" was particularly rich and luxurious; he was arrested for dealing in forged banknotes. Daliah Kaufman, "Naval – Righteous or Self-Righteous: a Hebrew Adaptation of *Tartuffe* by Moliere in the Enlightenment Period", *Bamah*, 105–6, 1986, 38–49 (Hebrew); David Veksler, *Naval – the Zaddik or the Hypocrite*, Lembourg, 1874.

[20] Many adaptations/translations – that of Avraham Shlonsky (Habima, 1932), the adaptation by Chaim Hefer and Yossef Milo (Cameri, 1950), the translation by Natan Alterman (published in 1967 and staged by the Haifa Municipal theatre, 1970), the adaptation by Edna Shavit (Beer Sheba Stage, 1974) as well as her adaptation and direction of *On Frivolity and Hypocrisy* (Beer Sheba Municipal Theatre, 1986) – attack the religious establishment, which is identified with the image of Tartuffe, but the plays' components (set, costumes, props, music, etc.) are foreign and set in the past.

[21] Dan Urian, "Adaptations and Translations of *Tartuffe* into Hebrew", *Bamah*, 104, 1986, 73. (Hebrew)

[22] All quotations are from an interview I carried out with Yehoshua Sobol: Dan Urian, "*Tartuffe* in the Theatre, 1664–1985", *Iton 77*, 62, March 1985, 41. (Hebrew)

The translation has a deliberately enlightened hue – Sobol wished to translate it "in a way in which the author Y. L. Gordon would have translated it during the period of the Jewish enlightenment [*Haskala*]. We are, after all, living today in a sort of enlightenment period and a struggle with the forces of darkness." (*ibid.*) The reference to Gordon (1830–1892) is not coincidental. Among other things, Gordon wrote pointed satires about the rabbis. In his famous article "Wisdom for Fools" he attacked these "mistaken fools" over the minutiae of their laws:

> If the religion of Israel is really dependent upon hair – long sidelocks [...] an untrimmed beard, the hat on your heads and the rag covering your wives' and daughters' heads; if the principal business of fearing heaven is the way you eat or wash your hands [...] we have no part in it and reject them.[23]

In Sobol's version, Tartuffe is engaged in returning secularists to the religious fold and represents religious hypocrisy. In order to avoid misdirection of his barbs, Sobol opens the play with a masked dance, including masks of religious politicians and noted rabbis of the 1980s. The translation "Jewishizes" all the religious expressions in the play and adds many additional ones. Tartuffe is nicknamed "the *kashrut* supervisor", "a kosher chicken"; he talks incessantly about "the will of God", makes the "blessing over food" and when he inadvertently hiccups he immediately cries "Praise the Lord", and compares his desire for Elmire with "the love of God"[24] When Orgon offers him all his property he modestly accepts it "if that is God's will, may He be blessed" (p. 65). The "ultra-Orthodox Jewishizing" of Tartuffe reaches a peak in his seductive speech to Elmire, in which he attempts to overcome her fear that giving way to her desires would be a transgression of God's laws:

> There is no greater expert than I in granting *kashrut* certificates.
> The law truly forbids certain pleasures,
> but he who, like me, swims freely in the sea of Jewish law –
> will find many ways to get along with the Torah.

The Text in Molière's play is:

> [...] je sais l'art de lever les scrupules.
> Le Ciel défend, de vrai, certains contentements
> Mais on trouve avec lui des accommodements.

---

[23] Yossef Klausner, *A History of the New Hebrew Literature*, Vol 4, Jerusalem, Achiassaf, 1963, 335, 338–39. (Hebrew)
[24] Molière, *Tartuffe*, Hebrew version: Yehoshua Sobol, Tel Aviv, Or-Am, 1985, 53.

Selon divers besoins, il est une science
D'étendre les liens de notre conscience. (*Tartuffe* 4, 5)

From Satire to "Crumbling" Realism

An important and paradigmatic component in religious representation in secular theatre is the choice of genre. Several studies, including those of Georg Lukács and Fredric Jameson, perceive the genre as an organization of fictional material based on "a social contract" between author and target audience.[25] It is clear that the dominant genre employed to illustrate the secular/religious schism is that of satire. The advantages of satire in regard to pointed criticism of one group by another are obvious. It is generally staged by the fringe theatre and aimed at a restricted audience who identify with the world outlook of the play's creators. This also lessens the likelihood of intervention by the censor that this type of text tends to attract. Satire contains its own "negation"; it is pointed but nonetheless "only" satire and as such is permitted to go to extremes. Satire also tends toward a clear intertextuality in that it relates to well-known public figures as well as to other texts familiar to the audience. This tendency facilitates a cognitive, definitive and interpretative involvement in the "debate", as demanded by the text, without harming the enjoyment of a theatrical event. We can add to this the enjoyment gained from mocking the religious "Other", which is also a way of overcoming necromancy and of dwarfing figures from the Israeli secularist's stockpile of horrendous characters. The intensification of the conflict in extra-theatrical reality is what led, as we shall see, to "the liberation" of the religious image from the "ghetto" of satire and shaped it towards "realism".

The secular/religious conflict first appeared on the small stages of the Israeli theatre, in satires staged by Ha'Kumkum [the kettle] and Ha'Matateh [the broom] theatres.[26] The religious establishment and its sacred accoutrements were the targets of satiric barbs *à la Tartuffe*. For example, in the sketch "The Judge's Seat" (Ha'Kumkum, 1928), the stage directions instruct the religious character to stroke the hand of the female

---

[25] Tony Bennett, *Outside Literature*, London and New York, Routledge, 1990, 78–114; Fredric Jameson considers the genre as an organisation based upon "agreement" between the author and a particular target audience: Fredric Jameson, *The Political Unconscious: Narrative as a Socially Symbolic Act*, Ithaca, Cornell University, 1981, 106.

[26] David Alexander, *'Ha'Kumkum', the Beginning of Satirical Theatre in Israel*, M.Sc. thesis, Department of Theatre Arts, Tel Aviv University, 1975. See: David Alexander, *The Jester and the King, Political Satire in Israel: A Temporary Summary, 1948–1984*, Tel Aviv, Sifriat Poalim, 1985. (Hebrew); and see: David Alexander, "State and Religion in Israel: a Satirical Point of View", *Assaph*, 4, 1988, 139–48.

servant "Blessing"; he also arranges for his brother to get "a job with a small wage". Another satirical theatre, the Theatre Club, continued along the same lines, being anti-clergy from the outset. Its very first program (1957) featured a quartet of Jewish gravediggers who sang "The Good Guys", dedicated to the religious burial society of the *Hevra Kaddisha*, with whom one must: "book a place well in advance/a really good position, in the centre [...] but you'll also have to pay a little/if you pay cash/or at least a no more than two month post-dated cheque/we shall, perhaps, comb the beard/and we'll also wash our hands in your honour." It was also possible to bend the religious laws for a suitable fee: "If a client happens to be uncircumsized –/we'll bury him like a donkey./ But if he has an uncle who 'jingles' [gives bribes]/he'll be accepted into Abraham's covenant."

Following the success of the *Hevra Kaddisha* ditty "and perhaps because of the concomitant tension in Jerusalem in the struggle against the religious",[27] *Datiada* [Religious Parade] (1958) was written. The show was staged against a background of the coalition crisis over the question of "Who is a Jew", at a time when David Ben-Gurion – then prime minister, was attempting unsuccessfully to define a Jew for the requirements of registration by the Ministry of the Interior, and thus determine eligibility under "The Law of Return" through a simple declaration. *Datiada* was a daring show for its time, more for its theatrical signs than its contents, which were fairly moderate in approach. The four actors were dressed in skullcaps as ultra-Orthodox Jews. One of them appeared on stage grasping the *tsitsit* [fringes] of his *tallith* [ritual prayer shawl] in his hand, which he had cut one by one in the course of singing one of the choruses. One of the songs was dedicated to the rabbi who had been caught embezzling and who also performed "miracles.":

> If I only had a thousand pounds/I would at once show you a trick/for two thousand in cash/you could rule over the Yemenite kingdom/the angel Gabriel suddenly whispered: 'buy the rabbi a new Dodge car'/who knows the rabbi?/But one day a policeman appeared/and magic could no longer help/for the rabbi is now a gaolbird.

The program aroused controversy and one of the secular newspapers even headlined it as "Anti-Semitism on the Hebrew Stage."[28]

Status Quo Vadis, staged by the Haifa Municipal Theatre in 1973, was the first play performed on a public stage (albeit the smaller auditorium) that featured the secular/religious divide and it reveals a recurring

---

[27] Noted by Dan Almagor.
[28] R. Azariah, "Every Night", *Ma'ariv*, 6 March 1958. (Hebrew)

pattern in which the theatre text constitutes an almost provocative stimulus for public debate. Representatives of the two opposing camps in the political conflict, at both local and national level, added greatly to its claims and its effect through articles in the printed and electronic media. The play is a theatrical adaptation of Shulamit Aloni's book about the conflict from the legal point of view. The playwright, Jehoshua Sobol, performed an extensive study of religious law, held interviews with public figures and with those members of the public who had been forced to undergo "ritual" ceremonies, such as conversion or *Haliza* [release from a widow's obligation to marry the brother of her late husband]. The songs in the play were based upon parliamentary speeches or newspaper reports. Documentary sources provided one of the mechanisms used to depict the schism and it was also influenced by the tradition of documentary theatre currently being staged in several European and American theatres. The program notes for the play included a section from the writings of the German playwright Peter Weiss on documentary theatre, mainly criticism regarding the covering-up of facts, distortion and lies; Edna Shavit, who directed the play, defined her work as "spoken journalism."[29] The "uncovered" facts related, for example, to the noted *status quo* agreement signed by David Ben-Gurion in 1947 which, according to this version, was extorted from the Zionist administration when the Agudat Israel ultra-Orthodox political party threatened to leave the Jewish national unity leadership upon testifying before the United Nations investigation committee.[30] One of the sketches in the play presented the agreement between Ben-Gurion and the religious factions over the exemption of *yeshiva* [College for study of the Torah] students from military service, as the result of religious fraud. Another mechanism employed in organising the play's material was to use the satiric-cabaret genre. Documentary and satire were combined. To use terms suggested by Elizabeth Burns, the documentation served as conventions of "authenticity" ("reflecting" social reality), while the

---

[29] Miriam Tao, "Status Quo Vadis – Theatre Nonetheless", *Davar*, 8 February 1973. (Hebrew)
[30] In June 1947, the Executive Committee of Agudat Israel, the non-Zionist religious party, received a letter from the chairman of the Jewish Agency, David Ben-Gurion, the political leader of the *yishuv* [the Jewish community in Palestine during the period of the British Mandate], offering a number of promises with respect to public control of religious matters in the soon-to-be-established state. The letter promised that: (1) Saturday would be set aside as the national day of rest; (2) dietary laws (*kashrut*) would be observed in all kitchens under government auspices; (3) religious courts would maintain exclusive jurisdiction over marriage and divorce laws; and (4) the existing autonomous religious educational systems would be recognised by the future state."
Eliezer Don-Yehiya, "The 'Status Quo' Agreement as a Solution to Problems of Religion and State In Israel", Charles S. Liebman and Eliezer Don-Yehiya, *Religion and Politics in Israel*, Bloomington, Indiana University Press, 1984, 32.

"rhetorical" conventions (that shaped the "theatricality")[31] leant toward cabaret: sketches, ditties with music by Yossi Mar-Chaim, inter-connecting scenes "propelled", according to the director, by much movement, hats, cloaks, sticks, all borne by actors dressed in everyday attire. These combinations created a text that guided the spectators to "concentrate" on the documents or factual stories as if they were "study cases", and to gain an insight into religious coercion from them; while the cabaret supplied the amusement as well as being a means of lessening possible objections from the government and its institutions – which were raised anyway.

Despite this, *Status Quo Vadis* was nonetheless quite restrained, particularly from the theatrical point of view – no religious icons were present on the stage nor other signs of the ultra-Orthodox world; even the costumes were of non-religious cabaret types. Sobol also stated that he was not seeking an "anti-religious evening", but a show "based on respect for belief and believer – it was intended to attack hypocrisy, the erosion of civil rights and the establishing of our lives according to elements of religious law that had lost all meaning and become outmoded."[32] The sketches and songs mainly depict situations of religious hypocrisy. They examine the main argument for forcing the religious laws governing personal status upon the secular population: preserving "the unity of the nation" – and present it as relinquishing something without gaining anything in exchange. The play features the tale of a teacher in the religious state school system who is fired from her job after she marries a non-religious Jew. The religious anachronism is demonstrated in the tales of ritual release of war widows from their obligation to remarry, as well as in the tales of *mamzerim* [one born of an illicit, e.g. adulterous union] and the difficulties encountered in mixed marriages. One of the songs, for example, takes its inspiration from a newspaper report which quoted a rabbi by the name of S. A. Greenberg who claimed, apparently in all seriousness, that an illegitimate child has inferior genes to those of any ordinary Jew:

> a sort of gene
> sort of different
> sort of little
> and it will give our son
> [...]
> a free ticket straight to hell.

---

[31] Elizabeth Burns, *Theatricality: a Study of Convention in the Theatre and in Social Life*, New York, Harper and Row, 1973, 40–121.

[32] Emanuel Bar-Kedma, "The Skullcap and Coercion", *Yediot Aharonot*, 10 February 1973. (Hebrew)

Since the 1970s the secular/religious divide has appeared many times on the satirical stage, with its religious stereotypes becoming particularly intensified in the 1980s; an extremism familiar not only in such plays but also in the theatrical semiotic system that was chosen for this purpose: costume, hair, props and music all combined to create a particularly negative image. There have been innovations in the addition of archetypes in recent years, such as the Zionist-religious settler in the occupied territories or the *Sephardic* [oriental] ultra-Orthodox type. Texts were written by such writers as Hanoch Levin, Yehoshua Sobol, Yossef Mundi, Daniel Lapin and Yoni Lahav, Kobi Niv, Ilan Hatzor, Ilan Sheinfeld, Orli Castel-Bloom and others. The most prominent writer of theatrical texts to deal with the ultra-Orthodox and the Orthodox Zionist is Shmuel Hasfari. *The Last Secularist* (1986) by Hasfari appears to say all that the genre can say on the subject, as a dystopic vision in which only one secular person remains in a totally ultra-Orthodox Israel. Hasfari does not restrict himself to a condemnation of religious coercion. He bitingly discloses the cultural contradiction that divides Israeli society – between the Zionist "civil religion"[33] and the ultra-Orthodox culture. This cabaret derides the "civil religion" in the face of its believers, who are no less than the spectators in the auditorium. The actors in *The Last Secularist* are dressed like ultra-Orthodox Jews participating in a cabaret that explores the establishment of the ultra-Orthodox State of Judea upon the ruins of the secular State of Israel. In one of the scenes Chupchik appears; he was once an entertainer and now demonstrates his devotion to religion. Chupchik is required, like other famous individuals who "returned to the fold" (including Uri Zohar), to use his secular past to deride the very same culture which created him, and in order to do so he is instructed to play the national anthem *Hatikva* by farting:

> Chupchik, who found fame for his wondrous ability to produce tunes from any part of his body; and who understood the hint and gave up his faith. He will demonstrate here a recently developed new number [...] the artist will play us something spine-chilling – *Hatikva*, the State's national anthem that we all remember.

In order to lessen Chupchik's last remaining doubts, the ultra-Orthodox desecrate the sanctity of the civil religion. They deride its symbols, the flag of the State of Israel and the sound of the siren announcing Remembrance Day for those who fell in the wars of Israel.

---

[33] As the Zionist culture is termed by Don-Yehiya and Liebman: Eliezer Don-Yehiya, Charles S. Liebman, "The Dilemma of Reconciling Tradition, Culture and Political Needs: Civil Religion in Israel", note 30, 41–56.

More than in any of the earlier texts, *The Last Secularist* "discloses" the hypocrisy of the religious, revealing it in different ways, and in their sexual connection, such as presenting the "modesty overseer" as a lesbian who preys upon prostitutes; and in songs about the ultra-Orthodox young men who cannot control their sexual urges:

> For beneath the black *kapota* [coat] and the *streimel* [fur-brimmed hat]
> For beneath the beards the men are still burning
> And when a hint of bum is displayed and when a breast is revealed
> Thousands here will "stand erect" with money in their hand.

The Last Secularist makes particular use of Israeli religious radical concepts, with the common denominator for all these groups, according to research by Aviezer Ravitzky, being that it "sees contemporary life in the Jewish [Zionist, D.U.] State, in Israel as if they were in the Diaspora."[34] In the dream of redemption of several of these groups there is no place for a secular society, including kibbutz members or Arabs, of whom only one "item" remains in the play; it is pertinent only to a State ruled by religious fundamental law.

Shmuel Hasfari also wrote *Kiddush* (1985, 1995). This is a realistic play depicting the secular/religious schism from the "anthropological" aspect without any secular figures appearing on stage. A more extreme approach to presenting the schism can be seen in the abandonment of the "circuitous strategies" (of adapting drama from translated repertoire and of satire) and a trend to more realistic staging of the conflict from the middle of the 1980s.[35]

Hasfari wanted to show on stage the change that had occurred among those same Zionist Jews who were attempting to bring together the two religions – the traditional and the Zionist. He follows the ritual Sabbath eve blessings in one such family and depicts a process showing the rising political power of the group to which it belongs, accompanied by extremism and the realisation of a dream of power. Following the Six Day War, the religious father says:

> When I think about my son becoming a paratrooper in the holy places: in Nablus, Hebron, the city of the fathers ... Jericho ... it's like a dream.[36]

The theatrical chronicle *Kiddush* is a synecdochical "reflection" of a family representing a particular social group, a process which Horowitz

---

[34] Aviezer Ravitzky, *Messianism, Zionism and Jewish Religious Radicalism*, Tel Aviv, Am Oved, 1993, 203. (Hebrew)

[35] see also Yossef Bar-Yossef, *Boochie*, 1984; and Sami Michael, *Twins*, 1989: both produced by the Haifa Municipal Theatre.

[36] Shmuel Hasfari, *Kiddush*, Tel Aviv, Or-Am, 1990, 57. (Hebrew)

and Lissak described as "change from politicisation of religion to religionisation of politics, that also involves theologisation of ideology."[37] The father, a shabby religious clerk who in the past had also voted for a secular party, demonstrates in his own way the revolution that had begun among the religious-Zionists. The realistic imaginary world depicts this process and the end of the play illustrates his abandonment, his internal contradiction and the hopelessness of his chances. The son not only becomes secular but also emigrates from Israel to the U.S.A., thus abandoning both religions – the Jewish and the Zionist. The end of the play is therefore broken up into almost Beckettian scenes, in which the characters speak to themselves, to tape recorders, or on the telephone: an end in which those same grotesque elements proliferate that had accompanied the characters from the beginning of the play as background music, now take over the performance.

A Protest Melodrama

Several critics and journalists have noted, apparently in condemnation, that *Fleischer* is "a melodrama". In the generic hierarchy of those who determine "good taste" in Israeli theatre, melodrama has been relegated to the lower rungs, near that of satire. Nonetheless, it is perceived as "reflecting" reality, or only slightly distorting it, due to its emotional filters. There are many signs that attest to its melodramatic quality and even the violin music by Rafi Kaddishsohn, that "sets the mood" of the play upon the darkened stage, adds to this characterisation. The choice of this genre to represent the belligerent attitude of one particular group (secularist) to another group (ultra-Orthodox) is indeed effective. *Fleischer* is a protest theatre text with many aims: to create political awareness, to examine values, to reveal injustice and support changes … the medium can be satire, a propaganda play, but also, according to J. L. Smith – melodrama.[38] The melodrama, as a protest play, features a cross-bearing protagonist fighting immense corruption. He must cast out all doubt, devote himself to the cause and fight with all those same extremist forces that symbolise evil. Ira Hauptman argues that in this respect melodrama is "a sort of religious drama […] It is symbolic drama that sees life as a battlefield between good and evil."[39] As no compromise between such conflicting views of good and evil is possible in melodrama, it always ends in either victory or failure. Each of these possibilities serves to enlist new faithful to the cause. Victory can cause pleasure

---

[37] Horowitz, Lissak, note 3, 98.
[38] James L. Smith, *Melodrama*, London, Methuen, 1973, 72.
[39] Ira Hauptman, "Defending Melodrama", *Melodrama, Themes in Drama*, 14, James Redmond (ed.), Cambridge, Cambridge University Press, 1992, 283.

while failure raises righteous anger over the injustice in the world, without our taking the slightest element of blame upon ourselves – and this is indeed how *Fleischer* ends.

As the playwright Yigal Even-Or notes, *Fleischer* is the story of:

> An elderly couple, holocaust survivors, who own a butcher shop near their home [:...] When they arrived in the neighbourhood shortly after the War of Independence (1948), it was a good neighbourhood inhabited by people who "had founded the State". Thirty-five years later the neighbourhood is decaying. The younger generation has left and not returned [...] Without their even noticing it, an ultra-Orthodox neighbourhood has been built under their very noses [...] they obtain loans and renovate the butcher shop, paying out a lot of money for the appropriate permits [...] *they try to stay afloat like survivors on a life-raft, on the sea of the ultra-Orthodox that rages around them, threatening to drown them* (my emphasis, D.U.) [...] (they) even attempt a partial return to Orthodox Judaism, in order to attract the ultra-Orthodox customers. The butcher shop remains empty and boycotted.[40]

The melodrama ends in a victory for the ultra-Orthodox – the death of the butcher shop owners when the shop burns down, the adoption of their retarded son by the ultra-Orthodox community rabbi, and the entire neighbourhood being taken over by the "black-clad" community.

The author accompanied the play with interviews in which he presented his approach as having been influenced by Molière's *Tartuffe*:

> I reached the conclusion that we are all suffering from an optical illusion. We present the security problem as of national prime importance. However, this is a simply and easily solved problem in comparison with that of religious coercion. The war with the Arabs is a territorial problem that will eventually be solved. The real problem with which we shall have to deal is less easy to solve.[41]

Even-Or sees the play as being about "Orgon weakness", as expressed by the secular side of the secular/religious struggle:

> Have you ever tried to ask a secularist if he believes in God? What does he reply? He doesn't reply, he begins to stammer [...] The ultra-Orthodox for some reason live completely at peace with this conflict. They say: "We aren't interested in why he wants to eat non-kosher meat, we shall force him to eat kosher". The secularists, however, are at odds with this, for they secretly see the ultra-Orthodox as sort of real Jews on

---

[40] In the program notes to *Fleischer*. (Hebrew)
[41] Daniella Fisher, "Cultural War", *Al Ha'Mishmar, Hotam*, 21 May 1993. (Hebrew)

the one hand, while on the other hand they constantly attempt to understand them and not to injure their feelings.[42]

While Even-Or did not intend a "documentary play", *Fleischer* nonetheless accurately reflects the secular/religious conflict. Research by Naomi Struch and Shalom Schwartz examined the antagonism of the inhabitants of a "mixed" neighbourhood in Jerusalem, primarily by the secular and "traditionalists" towards the ultra-Orthodox. They reached the conclusion that "it is possible to discern a consistent pattern of greater antagonism towards the ultra-Orthodox, and a perception of tremendous differences in values."[43] The proximity to the ultra-Orthodox was perceived by those interviewed as "threatening"; there was a significantly high level of support for "those who try to convince others not to sell their apartments to the ultra-Orthodox." (*ibid.*) As already stated, Israeli theatre approaches "reality" in its theatrical referents. The base of Pavis's "iceberg" (see Introduction), therefore, is close to the visible tip, which is the theatrical text itself, thereby possibly turning it into a "placard", as the critics claim; this does not, however, diminish the power of its influence on the audience.

From the theatrical aspect the play, which has only one set – the butcher shop – and few characters, presents a process of ultra-Orthodoxization, with the butcher shop appearing to become kosher and a suitable sign hung up to testify to this change; the number of ultra-Orthodox figures increases and the secular characters change their behaviour: they wear skullcaps, head scarfs, and carry out the various ritual commandments. The play's ultra-Orthodox *dramatis personae* are shaped similarly to those of satire and are clearly stereotypic. They are defined from their first appearance and their future behaviour is predictable. They have no past, unlike the secular figures who are "awarded" biographies, for in the past they fought and were wounded for the State, or educated their children according to Zionist values; and this serves to emphasize the sense of injustice done to them by the religious. Among the ultra-Orthodox, Hund (=dog; his name shocks some of the spectators, particularly the religious among them) is an especially negative figure due to his actions in ridding the neighbourhood of its secular inhabitants. He is dressed in black (a coat in the heat of August) and hypocritical: "Both in black and a lawyer." In several scenes he constitutes a physical negative caricature – for example when he hunches over to count the payment that he received from Fleischer to purchase a *kashrut* certificate.

---

[42] Neri Livneh, "I'm an anti-Semite?", *Hadashot*, 11 June 1993. (Hebrew)

[43] Naomi Struch, Shalom Schwartz, "Perception of the Conflict with the ultra-Orthodox, Perception of their Basic Values and the Antagonism of the non ultra-Orthodox towards the ultra-Orthodox", *Megamot*, Vol. 32, No. 1, 1989, 17. (Hebrew)

The play makes dozens of anti-Semitic statements from the very first moment: "God preserve me from the Jews"; "They (the ultra-Orthodox, D.U.) are stealing our country from under our noses"; "Even beasts of prey have souls. Not them"; "Soon the entire country will be theirs..." (a remark received with applause by the audience). The many references contrast the "Zionist civil religion" with the Jewish tradition – such as Fleischer using the frame surrounding his certificate of valor from the War of Independence to frame the *kashrut* certificate that he has purchased.

The importance of this play lies in its reception. Its great success appears to be the result of the social circumstances of the conflict. Watching the play elicited great involvement on the part of the audience, who laughed a lot at the anti-religious jokes and applauded several times. One of the performances which I attended was staged the day after the Jerusalem municipal elections, in which the ultra-Orthodox parties had achieved great success. To the audience at the Haifa Municipal theatre this was an opportunity to express concern and hatred, through laughter, whispered agreement and much applause. Amir Orian – a critic – described the events in the auditorium at another performance: "The same evening laughter was released and cries of agreement were sounded, and the moment when Fleischer said: 'they [the ultra-Orthodox, D.U.] will just touch them and the government will fall', the spectators murmured a concerted groan of 'amen'."[44] Zaharirah Charifai, who played the role of Berta in *Fleischer*, defined his relationship with the audience very clearly: "I have played this role over one hundred times. The audience accepts it because we are carrying out an action on its behalf and venting all those expressions of anger that the secular have against the religious."[45]

The play raised objections among politicians and members of Parliament (including secularists) who saw it as overflowing with self-hatred and racialism. Many "secondary texts"[46] contributed to disseminating its message: articles and information in the press and electronic media turned it for a time into a controversial subject, bringing its message to hundreds of thousands. The play itself is considered to be highly successful, with the number of spectators to date having reached 56,264. It was nominated among the top ten successful plays for 1993 and 1994.[47]

---

[44] Amir Orian, "Religious Ritual and the Tea Ritual", *Ha'Ir*, 4 June 1993. (Hebrew)

[45] "May God save Us from the Religious", *Two Cities*, 7 January 1994. (Hebrew)

[46] Tony Bennett's study on James Bond is a theoretical formulation of the function of "secondary texts" and their influence on "primary" reception of the text, based on advertising and critics' items. Tony Bennett, "Text and Social Process: the Case of James Bond", *Screen Education*, 41, 1982, 3–15.

[47] *Summary of Activities by Public Institutions of Culture and Art in Israel in 1993*, Tel Aviv, Administration for Culture and Art, The Council for Culture and Art, July 1994, 36. (Hebrew)

Analysis of a questionnaire handed out to audiences attending *Fleischer*[48] shows that the types of spectators who saw the play were similar to those attending theatre in general: mainly native Israelis of western origin, well-educated (high-school and above; 36.2% had academic degrees). Among those who responded to the questionnaire the great majority (87.5%) had attended other plays during the season and were active theatre-goers. An important finding was that they defined themselves as secular (absolute secularist – 54.6%; traditionalists – 32.9%). Those spectators who were apparently not influenced by some of the negative criticism by theatre critics agreed that the play transmits a social message (94%). A great many of them believed that the play provides a faithful representation of contemporary Israel (51.3%) while another section found a parallel between Israeli reality and what was shown on stage (38.8%). Another interesting finding was that over half the spectators during the course of the performance felt that they identified with the secular characters. Religious spectators sensed such hostility and even hatred directed towards them that they felt inclined to "take off their skullcaps."

The studies quoted at the beginning of this chapter as characterizing the secular/religious schism, tend towards playing down its dichotomous force and do not match the fictional scene staged by Israeli theatre, particularly from the 1970s on. Presentation of the religious stereotype in the theatre in its negative form, in an institution located high up in the Israeli cultural hierarchy and before a very large audience of spectators who not only object, but even appear to participate in the ritual of exorcising the demon, presents a strong antagonism on the part of one group of theatre-goers towards the ultra-Orthodox, the Zionist-religious and the oriental ultra-Orthodox.[49]

Since the 1970s there has been an increase in the frequency of such expressions by researchers, journalists and artists, who perceive the schism as a dichotomy. This is not only because of the increased number of incidents relating to the secular/religious divide, but is due to the

---

[48] The questionnaire was presented at two performances of *Fleischer* at Z.O.A. House on May 8th and 10th, 1994. 152 out of the 543 members of the audience completed the questionnaire, some during the intermission and most at the end.

[49] Prominent among the researchers who "read" the reality of this dispute differently, and more similarly to that presented in the theatre, is Gershon Weiler: "The Jewish religion and the existence of this State are a contradiction in terms, and therefore no State that is essentially Jewish is in fact possible." Gershon Weiler, *Jewish Theocracy*, Tel Aviv, Am Oved, 1976, 9. (Hebrew) A similar viewpoint is held by Yossef Agassi and Uri Huppert. Akiva Orr believes that "the struggle over defining the Jewish identity [...] throughout the years has been carried out in an emotional and aggressive manner, with each side perceiving the other side's opinions as a threat to their very existence and character." Akiva Orr, *The UnJewish State, the Politics of Jewish Identity in Israel*, London, Ithaca Press, 1983, 232.

much improved means of reporting, mainly through television, that has made "the theatre of life" a public possession, particularly for those secularists who draw their information and drama from this source. The appearance of representatives of the religious parties on television and reporting of events connected with the conflict, mainly focus on the controversy over the Sabbath and the secular way of life: the use of private vehicles on Sabbath; Saturday football; Friday night and Saturday visits to the cinema and other places of entertainment; working on the Sabbath and shutting down the national transport; advertisements that show women provocatively dressed; religious control of secular education and its resources by a religious Minister of Education; various demands to separate men and women on buses and even in cemeteries; the conflict around archeological excavations ... all these and more strengthen a certain secular perception of the religious, and particularly of those politicians who represent them (and whose political status has increased in recent years), as a group who do not wish for a *status quo*. The ultra-Orthodox and religious are seen as flag-bearers of an ideology that wishes gradually to turn religious law into state law. Among other religious groups and groups of secularists, recent years have seen a re-definition of Judaism, differing greatly to that of the Orthodox conception. These have reached the various Israeli stages, particularly that of television which "stars" the religious politicians whose exploitation of the rules of the political game is seen by many as extortion. Televised events of the conflict such as that between the archaeologists (dressed like bronzed pioneers from the past) and the ultra-Orthodox (pale and garbed in black), are portrayed as a struggle between the forces of light and darkness. These are the factors that are involved in shaping the perception of the schism and turning it into a dichotomy. From many aspects religious presentation in the theatre is not an exceptional expression by a fringe group, nor is it restricted to an elite secular intelligentsia, for the audiences are more varied than this. It is, in fact, an expression of such strong frustration elicited by the religious "Other" among Jewish Israeli secularists that it has reached the point of "self-hatred".

2

SEEKING ONE'S IDENTITY

The story begins one autumn evening in 1968 at Kibbutz Ha'Ogen in Emek Hefer, where the experimental staging of a new play [...] *Ish Hassid Haya*, took place. The kibbutz members, mostly also members of Hashomer Hatzair [a leftwing Zionist movement], had been invited by the producer [Yaakov Agmon, D.U.], also a member of the same movement, into their beautiful auditorium to watch a new play, with a clearly religious title, whose set had been designed by Danny Karavan (Hashomer Hatzair of course) in the style of the decorated wooden beams of Polish synagogues. The play had of all things been written by a member of Maccabi Hatzair [Dan Almagor, D.U.], the son of one of the first members of Hashomer Hatzair in Poland, who had educated his son in a decidedly anti-religious spirit [...] The first half of the first experimental staging of the play at Ha'Ogen passed in a thin silence, causing tension among the playmakers. However, in the final moment of the first act, at the end of the tale of Gedalia the tar-spreader, the applause nearly brought the house down.[1]

A generation's doubts regarding its identity,[2] and changes in the "structure of feeling"[3] of a prominent sector in Israeli society, help to explain the peculiar success of the play *Ish Hassid Haya*, seen by over quarter of

---

[1] Dan Almagor, "*Sephardi* against *Ashkenazi*, or: How I did not write 'A Spanish Garden'", *Yediot Aharonot*, 11 September 1992; Yoram Kaniuk describes the "premiere" audience in Tel Aviv who "went overboard with enthusiasm." Yoram Kaniuk, "Hassidim and Hassidism on behalf of (*Ish Hassid Haya* at the Bimot Theatre)", *Davar*, 25 October 1968. (Hebrew)

[2] According to Karl Mannheim, under circumstances of especially swift social changes, certain generations develop an awareness, a way of life, that distinguishes them in particular from previous generations. Karl Mannheim, *Essays in the Sociology of Knowledge*, London, Routledge and Kegan Paul, 1952.

[3] The "structure of feeling". This concept, introduced by Raymond Williams, relates to the values shared by a particular group, class or society. It is a combination of cultural collective sub-conscious and ideology, expressed in different forms, such as song, fiction, theatre, architecture, fashions etc. Raymond Williams, *The Long Revolution*, Harmondsworth, Penguin, 1965, 64–65.

Williams credits the playwright with the ability to give expression to a consciousness common to himself and his target audience. He presents the "structure of feeling" as a term outlining "the continuity of experience from a particular work, through its particular form, to its recognition as a general form and then the relation of this general form to a period." R. Williams, (1968) *Drama from Ibsen to Brecht*, Harmondsworth, Penguin, 1973, 9.

a million spectators in Israel, with an English version on Broadway (*Only Fools Are Sad*, 1971) and various translated versions used by Jewish communities and schools in other countries. Such success can be comprehended only against the background of change that had begun taking place after the Six Day War, in the Israeli attitude to the Jewish component of their identity; in particular among those born in the 1930s – the "second generation". The play was part of the new pattern of "tradition" and *Yiddishkeit* that was beginning to be seen among secular Israelis.[4] These changes found their expression in *Ish Hassid Haya*, whose *structure* tended towards innovative experimental theatre and whose contents comprised elements from the Jewish past suitably adapted to contemporary times and audiences. According to the director Yossi Yzraely: "We knew that this production was different, but didn't pay much attention to its importance. The reaction of the audience at Kibbutz Ha'Ogen was the first sign that we had created a contraband play."

The Six Day War, and even before then the educational policy of Jewish studies in secular schools, had reinforced the change in approach to Judaism among various sectors of Israeli society, as described by Amnon Rubinstein:

> The gradual change in attitude to religion is not expressed in a rebirth of faith, but in a more sceptical examination of secular Zionist coercion, particularly its socialistic implications, in regard to the traditional-religious [...] Instead of denying the Diaspora, came longings for a world that had fallen in ruins [...] the Jewish *shtetl* [Jewish township] – the address to which all the anger and despair of nationalist Judaism in eastern Europe had been directed in the past – received a new and positive significance in Israeli awareness. Books, paintings and exhibitions immortalise its cultural uniqueness.[5]

---

[4] Differing from "religion" which "sees the commandments as one indivisible issue, undisputed and from which one cannot retreat", "tradition" according to Anita Shapira "sees them as a collection of customs [...] an optional system, one of many systems required by man," while "Yiddishkeit" is:

> A more hazy concept. It expressed an attitude to a social and cultural experience, connected to Jewish family life in the Diaspora. [...] "Yiddishkeit" is interested in the experiences of daily life, folklore and humour. It deals with the lifestyle of the simple Jew, and therefore emphasizes Jewish folk culture.

Anita Shapira, "Religious Motifs of the Labour Movement", *Zionism and Religion*, Shmuel Almog, Yehuda Reinhertz, Anita Shapira (eds.), Jerusalem, Zalman Shazar Centre, 1994, 304–5. (Hebrew)

[5] Amnon Rubinstein, "The Period after the Six Day War", *From Herzl to Gush Emunim and Back*, Jerusalem and Tel Aviv, Shoken, 1980, 106–8. (Hebrew)

Charles S. Liebman found among these groups (particularly "among some *Ashkenazi* Jews" [of European origin]) a tendency to adopt those concepts that suited them from the religious tradition: "but this is most certainly not the Orthodox religion. It is a search for symbols within the religious tradition, that are able to deliver a sense of meaning and purpose that the old symbols are no longer able to provide."[6]

The Six Day War was among those events which had an unmistakable effect on the "structure of feeling" of the second generation and thereby on Israeli society in general. Many, albeit hesitant, expressions of this can be found in one of the important documents to result from the war – *Siah Lohamim (The Seventh Day)*, in which several of the participants convey their change in attitude to Jewish history in expressions such as: "There was no-one, not even the toughest, who during the war didn't feel this something about the Jewish people."[7] There were also those who altered their viewpoints following the war. Yariv Ben Aharon, one of the founders of the "Shdemot Circle", and son of Yitzhak Ben Aharon, a leader of the Kibbutz Ha'Meuchad movement, recalled the crisis he underwent:

> With me this began immediately after the Six Day War. Encountering Israel's scenery, linked to memories from the Bible and the distress and shock created by every war [...] This date left a sort of "emptiness" in the leftist camp. Gush Emunim [the movement of the Zionist-religious settlers in the occupied territories] offered some type of solution but not what I was seeking [...] In my search for sources I was looking for something that would provide a way of life; that would have the vitality of human experience and of human and social action. I found it in the Talmudic-Midrashic literature, in Hassidism and also in the Bible. Not witty rationalisations. Something that reflected life. The search was a personal one that later became linked to my writing. The study, the language of the sources, the symbolism. I sensed that I was uncovering my inner self. In the society in which I lived. In the kibbutz. In the family. They did not applaud. As they saw it, I was stumbling [...] for this was a specific doctrine and perspective [...] It was a real crisis, for the attempts of these revolutionary generations to hide themselves from Jewish tradition, to describe a sort of new man, cut off in effect, making a new beginning in a new place, was destructive [...] There is no meaning in creating something new that does not learn from the old.

In the Hebrew theatre repertoire in Israel the "Judaism" component tended on the whole, particularly from the 1930s onward, toward *Yiddishkeit* – particularly in *shtetl* plays and works translated from

---

[6] Charles (Yeshayahu) Liebman, "Towards a Study of Popular Religion in Israel", *Megamot*, Vol. 23, No. 2, 1977, 105–6. (Hebrew)

[7] Avraham Shapira (ed.), *The Seventh Day*, published by a group of young members of the kibbutz movement, 1968, 276. (Hebrew)

Yiddish. Up until *Ish Hassid Haya* nothing had been staged that dealt with the Israeli Jewish identity other than a few satires whose barbs had been aimed at the religious establishment. In the decade prior to *Ish Hassid Haya*, from the 1960s, there had been only a very small number of "Jewish" plays. The four active theatres of that period (Habima, Cameri, Ohel and Haifa Municipal theatres) staged only 18 plays that could perhaps be placed in this category out of a total of 217 "original" plays.[8] Not one of these plays dealt directly with the Jewish nature of Israeli society. *Ish Hassid Haya*, therefore, provided the first theatrical discussion of the question of the Jewish identity of those who were seated in the auditorium.

A group of plays which could be termed "Jewish", by the playwrights Danny Horowitz, Yaakov Raz, Yossi Yzraely, Yehoshua Sobol, Aliza Elion-Israeli and others, staged from the beginning of the 1970s, were of a new generation. The majority of these plays were not part of the mainstream (with the exception of several of Yzraely's adaptations of Agnon) and most of them have been staged by the fringe theatres, in front of audiences which have remained small. The beginning of this process was in fact a production that reached a wide audience – *Ish Hassid Haya*. The common denominator between this and later plays lay in the disclosure, through textual structure and content, of the difficulties inherent in a dialogue between Israeli Jews and the Jewish tradition. Such a dialogue, due to a basic lack of knowledge and familiarity, is necessarily selective and hesitant and these plays tended toward the structurally experimental and fragmental. *Ish Hassid Haya*, like most of the plays dealing with the Judaism of Israeli Jews, is a theatrical text whose structure and content unfold this investigation of Judaism and its inherent difficulties and confusion.

Structure

From the point of view of theatrical structure, *Ish Hassid Haya* belongs to the American counter-culture. Dan Almagor, a contemporary of Yariv

---

[8] Based upon the following sources (all in Hebrew):
Giora Manor, "Original Plays Staged since 1948", *Teatron*, 15, April–May, 1965, 5.
Mendel Kohansky, "Plays from 1918–1974", *The Hebrew Theatre*, Jerusalem, Weidenfeld and Nicholson, 1974, 243–66.
Yehuda Gabai, (ed.), "List of Plays Staged by the 'Ohel' 1926–1969", *The Ohel Theatre: The Story of the Deed*, Tel Aviv, Mifal Tarbut v'Hinuch, 1983, 142–49.
Shlomo Shva, (ed.), *The First Seventy Years: The Story of Habima*, 1917–1987, Tel Aviv, Keter, 1987.
Hanni Zeligson, *The Habima Repertoire*, Tel Aviv, Habima: 1. 1918–1960; 2. 1961–1981.
40 Years of the Cameri Theatre, including repertoire, 1944–1984, Tel Aviv, Ha'Cameri, 1984, 45–53.
Israel Gur, "Haifa Municipal Theatre Repertoire, 1961–1981", *Bamah*, 90, 1982, 20–40.
Haifa Municipal Theatre 1961–1991, including 1961–1991 repertoire, Haifa, The Haifa Municipal Theatre, 1991.

Ben-Aharon, is also a member of an anti-traditionalist family, growing up in a home in which he was forbidden to go near a synagogue. He was drawn to Judaism while studying in the United States in the 1960s, in a period when many American Jews "discovered" their Jewishness and also gave it public expression in fiction and film. Almagor, like the director Yossi Yzraely, who also studied in the United States, was exposed to the influence and innovative approach of the American theatre of the 1960s. In regard to *Ish Hassid Haya*, they were both particularly affected by the performance staged by the Free Southern Theater, a mixed-race theatre, of a play entitled *In White America* by Martin Duberman. This "documentary" play about racial prejudice in the United States was highly appropriate to the "freedom summer" of 1964. It was minimalist theatre, somewhat along the lines of a *Story Theater* which was an innovative notion during those years.[9] "We began to talk a completely new theatrical language," says Yossi Yzraely, "there was a real revolution there."

Ish Hassid Haya was the initiative of the actor Shlomo Nizan, the only one of the participating actors to have come from a religious background, to have been educated in the religious schools and, so it would appear, to feel that the time was ripe to tell the Israeli theatre-goers tales from the Hassidic tradition. Nizan collected stories and reminiscences from his religious past, and also songs ("from home, from the *yeshiva*, from the youth movement"). These songs were unknown at the time and this was to be their first performance on a secular stage, in the spirit of *dvekut* [devoutness] that Nizan had brought with him "like a rabbi who sang with the Hassidim." The compilers, including Rabbi Shmuel Hacohen-Avidor, for several months found themselves unable to formulate a text for the play. Finally they remembered *In White America* and adopted its theatrical format – a text that was neither "conventional" nor "well-made":

> *Ish Hassid Haya* was composed of scenes, with no framework story, as a sort of anthological play, incorporating long tales, short tales, fables, anecdotes, jokes, sayings, songs and tunes, part of which were directed by Yossi Yzraely in a style reminiscent of the American Story Theater that had come into being in the United States at about that time.[10]

The Bimot theatre is not an establishment subsidized public theatre, which probably facilitated the choice of an experimental approach for the

---

[9] Dan Almagor described the performance he attended in Greenwich Village, New York, four years prior to writing/adapting *Ish Hassid Haya*. Dan Almagor, "'Lynch the Black Dog!' Screamed the Mob", *Ma'ariv*, 30 October 1964. (Hebrew)

[10] Almagor, note 1.

play. The genre – "an evening of Hassidic songs and tales" – does not feature a complete narrative, but a collection of short scenes organized and
directed toward the process of change being undergone by the audience.
Such an organization reveals the difficulty the playmakers had in presenting a clear statement and therefore their choice of a compilation of scenes
into a sort of anthology. Three organizational strategies are conspicuous
in the playmakers' intent toward their audience: to vary the story-telling
materials with sayings or songs; to mix serious and comic material; and,
in particular, to accompany the play with musical phrases and tunes.

The starting point for consolidating and directing the text was
one of rejection. This was "an impossible encounter" according to Yossi
Yzraely and Dan Almagor adds: "Everything that we had seen at
Habima about *shtetl* plays repelled us – scenery, costume, music."
Shlomo Nizan wanted to separate the "material from the structure...
a beard and sidelocks were not mandatory in order to enjoy a Hassidic
legend." The counter-culture is recognisable in the textual editing, which
was also influenced by Brechtian ideas: in organizing the play materials,
in the acting which contained elements of alienation, in the symbolistic
scenery, in the non-mimetic movement, in the modern costumes, in the
varied use of props; and in the music which constituted a mixture of the
authentic and the new. The influence of the counter-culture at the end of
the 1960s on American and European society, and its assimilation into
the majority culture, reveals how "an alternative" that is generally avant-
garde and directed at small groups of spectators, became "popular" and
reached such large audiences,[11] particularly in plays that moderated
their radical approach and message of social criticism, and even in plays
that were enlisted to disseminate conservative views. Although the
rhetorical conventions (which create the "theatricality", as defined by
Elizabeth Burns)[12] in *Ish Hassid Haya* are borrowed from the counter-
culture, the content of the play is an original adaptation of religious-
cultural-renewal. An explanation for the play's success can also be found
in that its "authenticating" conventions (those that, according to Burns,
"reflect" or "represent" the social reality) did not correspond to the
"authentic" social reality of East European Hassidism, but rather to
"a Reality Convention"[13] of "Diaspora Judaism" that this particular entertainment show had created for its audience in Israel at the end of the 1960s.

---

[11] Baz Kershaw, *The Politics of Performance, Radical Theatre as Cultural Intervention*, London
and New York, Routledge, 1992, 37–38.
[12] Elizabeth Burns, *Theatricality: a Study of Convention in the Theatre and in Social Life*, New
York, Harper and Row, 1973, 40–121.
[13] Gad Kaynar, "'Get Out of the Picture, Kid in a Cap?' On the Interaction of the Israeli
Drama and Reality Convention", *Theatre in Israel*, Linda Ben-Zvi (ed.), University of
Michigan, 1966, 285–301.

The vocabulary of theatrical semiotics used by *Ish Hassid Haya* can be understood from the sociosemiotic aspect (examining the social application of symbols in the theatre)[14] as an historical document capable of revealing the compelling changes taking place among an important Israeli social sector. There are no quotations or direct references that imitate the *shtetl* culture in its historical connections, partly because the ultra-Orthodox *shtetls* within the Israeli secular urban communities in which various versions of this culture had been retained (in Mea Shearim in Jerusalem or Bnei Brak near Tel Aviv), were perceived by the secular audience as a hostile or even hated image (Shlomo Nizan: "When I was a child the non-religious used to taunt me with the nickname *Aduk-fistuk* ['religious nut']"). The choice of a semiotic vocabulary close to the audience's own language, costume and musical concepts constituted a sort of declaration that demanded the rewriting ("deconstruction") of Jewish culture in its Israeli secular connection.

The "rhetorical" conventions of *Ish Hassid Haya* banned any similarity with the *shtetl* genre staged by Habima, the Ohel theatre and Broadway; theatres in which *shtetl* plays and musicals were accompanied by scenery that evoked an imaginary world (expressionistic or realistic), in which costumes were "recreated" and which introduced their audiences to "real" characters and the events in their lives. Yossi Yzraely, who had been afraid "to be swallowed up by this material" sought a play which would "distance the close approach" and in which the tension between old and new would be preserved throughout – an "avant-garde", "grey" and "alienated" play – Brechtian in style, without scenery ("and in this spirit he approached Danny Karavan and asked him to 'Make us a grey wall, no decorations whatsoever.'")[15] Karavan convinced him to choose a "symbolistic" backdrop hung with paintings found in Polish synagogues and these were the only "authentic" Jewish cultural "citations" in the play. The small and intimate stage featured several black wooden blocks as well as a few guitars (but no "Jewish" musical instruments) that could be used as different props (such as a rifle for the watchman). The blocks also served as drums to accompany the stories, thus determining the story rhythm and providing an element of tension. The costumes were contemporary and youthful in style, with the prominent element being corduroy trousers (and not jeans as reported by several of the critics in their headlines: "Hassidism in jeans" – an oxymoron in an era in which jeans were still perceived in Israel as "hippy" gear, just as long hair was considered to be a sign of a permissive

---

[14] Jean Alter, *A Sociosemiotic Theory of Theatre*, Philadelphia, University of Pennsylvania Press, 1990, 12–22.
[15] Emanuel Bar-Kedma, "Incarnations of a Melody", *Yediot Aharonot*, 11 October 1968. (Hebrew)

culture). To the dismay of several critics, the actors' movements abandoned the typical gestures of Hassidic dance, being devised instead as mime, accompanied by 1960s dance music like the Twist and changing positions of the wooden blocks. The actors who at first had had neat hairstyles, grew their hair until, à la Bob Dylan, they arrived at the huge Afro hairstyle, thereby reinforcing the overall concept of tradition being portrayed by new means.

"We created a theatrical language. From nothing!" noted Yossi Yzraely, "Mainly through the work of the actors", who changed identity and "split themselves" during the course of a story, enabling a "natural" transition from scene to scene.

The choice of an innovative structure for *Ish Hassid Haya* was an effective strategy as a "frame" for the contents of the play. The theatrical novelty was particularly noticeable in the "rhetorical" conventions. The playmakers realised that apparently incomprehensible and anachronistic contents, whose language and concepts are not understood, could none the less be understood and adapted – and even in an enjoyable way.

The play's success can also be understood against the background of change that began in the 1960s, a period when musicals and Israeli song festivals flourished. This was a period in which the highbrow culture also adopted styles, mainly musical, from "popular" culture. These changes led to new types of audiences, whose influence also made itself felt in the contents of *Ish Hassid Haya*.

Crossroads of Culture

Ish Hassid Haya is more than just an expression of rebirth of faith; it is a text that casts doubt on Zionist-socialist Judaism's denial of religion. It contains a different approach to the Diaspora – from rejection to yearning. Its search employs different means to those of the religious messianic zealots of Kiryat Arba or the secular hedonists of Dizengoff Street.[16] In this respect Dan Almagor considers "*Ish Hassid Haya* to be a sort of crossroads in the cultural and social history of Israel, bridging for the first time between traditional Jewish Hassidic material and Israeli youth and the secular public."

Not only the structure of the play, but also its materials enabled a dialogue between Israeli secularism and Jewish tradition. These constituted adaptations of original Hassidic and other sources (the writings of

---

16 Rubinstein, "From Herzl to Gush Emunim and Back", in: *From Herzl*, see: note 5, 126–27. Rubinstein considers the period following 1967 to have generated two separate paths: one, the parade of nationalist zealotry symbolised by the settlers in the occupied territories in Kiryat Arba; the other, the "good life" based upon a rise in the standard of living and the adoption of western fashions, symbolised by Dizengoff Street in Tel Aviv.

Martin Buber, Eliezer Steinman, Micha Yossef Berdichevsky, Mordechai Ben-Yehezkel ...), an anonymous tale (about the Baal Shem Tov's neighbour in the next world), the tale of Rabbi Nahman's journey to the Land of Israel, based on the legends of Rabbi Nahman of Braslav, and they even included an adaptation of a non-Hassidic story "borrowed" from the Tales of the town of Zefat. Rabbi Shmuel Hacohen-Avidor's promise that "this time we shall attempt to deliver Hassidism straight from the source," [17] did not turn out to be completely accurate; and it also created a scholarly dispute. Naftali Krauss was disturbed by the distorted sources as well as those contents which he considered to "caricature Hassidism through using a distorted mirror and stripping it of its soul."[18] Dan Almagor affirmed that writing the play had indeed been a process of trying to modify the adapted materials for a secular audience:

> I attempted to tell stories on stage. Most of the Hassidic tales that I had heard or read about had either been told or written in a complex, literary form, or suffered from non-realistic dramatization. I tried to re-tell the tales in a lighter vein, using humour – and foregoing the long descriptions of people, food, places and costumes [without "authentisizing" conventions, D.U.] that appear with high frequency in the tales of the *Shtetl*. This is how we arrived at the staccato, almost telegraphic style of several of the tales. In short, I wanted to clothe these ancient folk tales in modern dress, in a way that would draw the attention of a contemporary audience.[19]

The Hassidism in *Ish Hassid Haya* is a Jewish religious movement that maintains a balance between religion and humanism. Such Hassidism is comfortable for a secular (and uninformed) audience and in this version interrelationships and yearning for the Land of Israel play an important role. To this imagined Hassidism Martin Buber provided a decisive (albeit misleading) contribution as well as an important source for the playmakers. Buber's concept of Hassidism led to criticism by several researchers on the subject, who perceived a quite different picture of the movement, such as that of Rivka Schatz Uffenheimer:

> [...] from a reading of Hassidic sources, there is no basis for assuming that shifting the emphasis from study to devotion, was carried out for

---

[17] Program notes from *Ish Hassid Haya*, October 1968. (Hebrew)

[18] Naftali Krauss, "Ish 'Hassid' Haya...", *Ma'ariv*, 2 October 1969; Rabbi Hacohen-Avidor's reply was swift, "regarding Rabbi Nahman of Braslav's amazement and on *Ish Hassid Haya*", *Ma'ariv*, 9 October 1969; This did not settle the controversy and led to another reaction by Meir Urian, "Two Additional Reactions regarding *Ish Hassid Haya* and its Legends.", *Ma'ariv*, 23 October 1969. (in Hebrew)

[19] Emanuel Bar-Kedma, "The 'Hassidim' Go to Broadway", *Yediot Aharonot*, 12 July 1971. (Hebrew)

the social motives of bringing simple people closer to Judaism [...] nor were they to "make things easier" for the ordinary man, neither did they affirm his existence "as he is", according to Buber's reflections on Hassidic thought; on the contrary, they demanded the spiritual effort of man overcoming himself, more than the intellectual demands of study-ing the Torah.[20]

According to Yossef Dan, the stories and proverbs used by Buber to depict Hassidism created an image that conformed with his philosophy, but did not always suit Hassidism, which had been formulated by over one thousand volumes, most of which provided difficult reading. Although the Hassidic stories, like the melodies, had become sacred, this was not due to their religious contents, which did not constitute a reliable source from the religious Hassidic perspective. The ethical–theoretical interpretation of Hassidic tales, which removes them from their true con-text and from the literary genre to which they belong, leads to a distor-tion of this particular type of literature.[21] Moreover, Hassidic tales contain very little theoretical preaching and are mainly directed at extolling the *Zaddik* [lit. the righteous one; in this case the Hassidic rabbi – the religious leader] in question, with the moral of the story not being a Hassidic-ideological one, and the tale sometimes being told simply for the sake of enjoyment. These stories, which constitute the main body of the play, are in fact an illustration of Hassidism and contain very little which could teach about its theoretical perceptions, concepts and values.

An undercurrent in the play, of which the playmakers may have been unaware but which was of great significance to the audience, is the fact that between Zionism and Hassidism – as two reform movements – there existed and still exists acute hostility. The Hassidic attitude to *Eretz Israel* [the Land of Israel] is not unequivocal – although many Hassidics have gone far in their praise, and Rabbi Nahman of Braslav spent a year living in *Eretz-Israel*, only a few of the Hassidic sources show clear evidence of messianic movements that favoured emigration to the Land of Israel.

Voices: "I" and "Others"

The text of *Ish Hassid Haya* expresses a "structure of feeling" at the centre of which is the Israeli whose "self-esteem rose following the Six Day War in comparison to the period before the war."[22] From the collective point

---

[20] Rivka Schatz Uffenheimer, *Quietistic Elements in 18th Century Hassidic Thought*, Jerusalem, Magnes, 1968, 152. (Hebrew)

[21] Yossef Dan, *The Hassidic Story – Its History and Development*, Jerusalem, Keter, 1975, 60–61. (Hebrew)

[22] Kalman Benyamini, "National Stereotypes of Israeli Youth", *Megamot*, Vol. 26, No. 1, 1969, 369. (Hebrew)

of view the discourse after the war was homogeneous – finding its expression in the play, and addressing the "model spectator"[23] – basically an *Ashkenazi* male. Research by Yeshayahu Rim (1968), for example, reveals that children of both *Ashkenazi* and *Sephardi* [of oriental origin] descent considered the *Ashkenazi* to be the more faithful "Israeli" representative.[24] An innocent comment by one of the theatre critics, on the subject of the casting for *Ish Hassid Haya*, is equally revealing – Dov Bar-Nir found it difficult to believe that Lolik Levy, one of the actors was "a Yemenite; he looked more like a western-style beatnik."[25]

An explicit "Other" in the play is "Ivan" who is about to destroy the Jew (and is perhaps a sublimation of the sense of loss that accompanied the Arab threat just prior to the outbreak of the Six Day War), as is also the Nazi figure who appears in the scene that attempts to confront memories of the holocaust (possibly for the first time in front of such a wide audience and of all things on a stage devoted to light entertainment). The attitude to the implied "Others" in the text – Arabs, religious contemporaries of the audience, and women – is particularly interesting. The Arab "Other" in the play is transformed into a Cossack, in contrast to the transformation carried out by the native Hebrew culture at the beginning of the Jewish settlement period in Israel, when Eastern European characters such as the Cossack and the Ukranian peasant were transformed into images from the new land – Bedouin and *fellahin* [Arab agricultural labourer].[26] The play appears at first to have reverted to images and figures from the Diaspora past, except that these barely conceal the Arab "Other" and his contextual presence was clearly felt by an audience who in 1968 was still feeling the effects of the 1967 war. The *goy* [non Jew] in the play abducts Jews into the army and carries out a pogrom: "Ivan took many of them *this year* [my emphasis, D.U.], by fire and by water, by the sword and by choking." The *goyim* in the play try to humiliate the Jews and are attributed a degree of brutality not found in the Jews, as in the story of Rabbi Nahman of Braslav's emigration to Israel, which tells of the *Ishmaelim* [Muslim Arabs] who wanted to slaughter all the citizens of the town of Acre, in order "to make some room for themselves."

---

[23] The concept of the "model spectator" anticipated by theatrical performance is discussed in: Marco De Marinis, *The Semiotics of Performance*, translated: Áine O'Healy, Bloomington and Indianapolis, Indiana University Press, 1993, 165–71.

[24] Yeshayahu Rim, "National Stereotypes in Children", *Megamot*, Vol. 26, No. 1, 1968, 45–50. (Hebrew)

[25] Dov Bar-Nir, "*Ish Hassid Haya* at the Bimot Theatre", *Al Ha'Mishmar*, 25 October 1968. (Hebrew)

[26] A process noted by Ittamar Even-Zohar for the new Hebrew culture in Israel that exchanged the Cossack for a Bedouin and the Ukranian peasant for a *fellah*. Ittamar Even-Zohar, "The Growth and Consolidation of a Local and Native Hebrew Culture in *Eretz Israel*, 1882–1918", *Catedra*, 16, 1980, 175. (Hebrew)

Ivan (or the *Ishmaelite*) is equated to an Arab character in the eyes of the Jewish Israeli spectator who, according to the research of Kalman Benyamini, perceives him as "very negative and very bad."[27] The answer to these attacks of "Others" against the Jews is one of force – like the commandment "to grow" featured in one of the sketches, particularly in the demand for vengeance in the holocaust scene. An additional image of the "Other" – "the religious person" – differs from the "real" image as that involved in social and political conflict with the secular audience, unlike an earlier play by Dan Almagor *Datiada* (1958) which depicts the "religious" as ludicrous and corrupt. In *Ish Hassid Haya* the religious character is a figure from Buber's version of the Hassidic past, who has been remodelled for the needs of a secular audience hugging a past it did not experience. In this respect Naftali Krauss's criticism of one of the songs in the play, whose hero – Avram'le Melamed – is a useless failure, is informative. The song was adopted by anti-religious secular Israelis to ridicule the ultra-Orthodox:

> "Avram'le Melamed" [...] is currently being sung throughout the country by empty-headed, irresponsible kids, whenever a Jew with a beard and sidelocks passes them by on the street, exactly as the *shkuzim* [derogatory term for non-Jewish youth] used to do in the Diaspora, during a time that we no longer wish to remember. In this particular matter, of all things, *Ish Hassid Haya* has reached *authenticity* [my emphasis, D.U.], albeit a sad and superfluous authenticity, but one that deserves attention.[28]

An additional image of the "Other" in Israeli culture is a female one, particularly present in the 1960s. *Ish Hassid Haya* is in many respects a masculine text, replete with reports of war and victorious supermen. Women play a secondary and instrumental role in this world; and here too the text is at least accurate in depicting the inferior position of women in Hassidism.[29] Women in the stories and songs of the play are always on the fringe. The man is active and the woman, if indeed she manages to acquire any part at all, is the servant of her husband, or even cast in a ridiculous role: for example, the tale of the wife of Rabbi Menachem-Mendel of Rinov who sacrificed her place in the Garden of Eden in order to deliver bread to her poor and studious husband; or the song "Avram'le Melamed" in which a mother-in-law vents her anger on her son-in-law and Avram'le's wife is the bankrupt rich man's ugly daughter.

---

[27] Benyamini, note 22, 369.

[28] Naftali Krauss, see: note 18.

[29] Many of the authoritative Hassidic texts that address only men contain instructions on how to maintain a distance from women in order for the Hassid not to be distracted from God's work.

A Secular Judaism

The audience, who neither practice the commandments nor are familiar with the sources for most of the scenes of *Ish Hassid Haya*, above all find justification for a Jewish way of life that absolves them from carrying out the commandments and studying the Torah. The opening song is the motto – it is aimed at a generation and social group who have never known the prayer, the story or even the melody, but "only this we know –/ that once there was a melody" and the melody in the play is important because it "bridges" between the fumbling audience and the faded memories of a rich culture. Melodies therefore constitute the main component of the play and they are also adapted to suit contemporary musical tastes: jazz, blues, soul, and Brechtian ballads such as those of Kurt Weill.

Several of the sketches serve to moderate the contradiction that the director considers to be "actually the essence" of a secular play dealing with the contents of religious belief – they tell about characters whose entire energy is poured into their innocent faith, and not into carrying out commandments or studying the Torah. Two of the tales (that evoked pleasurable laughter from the audience) are about Rabbi Levy-Itzhak from Berdichev. In one of them the rabbi calls God to account – this is a "bankrupt" God who has permitted Ivan to abduct Jews into the Czar's army, to carry out pogroms against them, to kill and to rape … and so the *Zaddik* does not carry out the commandment to blow the *shofar* [holy ram's horn] and protests: "let Ivan blow the *shofar*!" In another story the same rabbi justifies the deeds of someone who smoked on the Sabbath, in that the wrongdoer had told the truth and not tried to excuse his sin with lies. The play also features two prayers – of a porter and a gooseherder, who return the audience's own ignorance back to the stage and link it to the tales of characters who don't even know how to pray. The story of a *tinok she'nishbah* [Talmudic term referring to status of a child who has been taken into captivity by non-Jews] and "the return of the son" is particularly reflective of the audience's attitude to Judaism: the tale is about a young Jew who has been abducted into the Czar's army, uprooted from his sources, and who can no longer remember anything except a white tablecloth, candles and an old man.[30] The audience, who have been severed from the sources of Judaism for

---

[30] Ironically, the story reflects the ultra-Orthodox attitude to the secular population in the 1990s – thus, for example, the Admor from Klausenberg explained the question of secular Jews who settled in Zion as follows: "The great majority of the holocaust children as well as native-born Israelis are like *tinok she'nishbah*, and what can one expect from them in the field of Judaism?" Cited from: Tamar El-Or, *"Tinokot she'nishbu*, Perception of Secularism among the ultra-Orthodox", *Megamot*, Vol. 34, No. 1, 1991, 111. Cited from the ultra-Orthodox weekly journal *Marve*. (Hebrew)

several decades, just like the abducted youth in the tale, "recreate" in the play a few distant memories from a forgotten tradition.

One story that became the subject of scholarly controversy (there were those who doubted its sources as a Hassidic tale) appears in the last sketch at the end of the first half, before the intermission, and a great deal of directorial work was invested in it. The tale is a kind of synecdoche: it tells of a secular group which uses slightly religious arguments to justify its growth and increase in strength so that it will be impossible to destroy it easily. This is the story of Gedalia the tar-spreader, who will be the Baal-Shem Tov's [Israel Baal-Shem Tov, founder of the Hassidic movement, 1698/1700–1760] neighbour in the next world, and who has no positive features: he is a giant, vulgar, ignores the commandments and eats enormous quantities of food. An enormous appetite constitutes his uniqueness. His father, a little nothing of a man, was burned by the Cossacks for refusing to kiss a cross, so Gedalia decided to eat to the extent that if he too will be set alight, this time the conflagration will be truly unmistakable:

> So they may see
> So they may know
> That a Jew does not burn
> Just for nothing
> So easily

The story of Rabbi Nahman's journey to the Land of Israel is intended to impart the importance of Israel to the Jews, as well as the change in attitude to the Diaspora following the Six Day War. Legitimization is given to any associations that assist in the return to the promised land – such as that of Rabbi Nahman. This scene features several signs of the time and expressions of the hybris that followed victory in the Six Day War: when Rabbi Nahman hears about the Napoleonic wars he is not put off by the dangerous journey and says: "Napoleon-Shmapoleon!" [an expression of disdain]. Immediately afterwards comes a story about Rabbi Moshe Teitelbaum's love for *Eretz Israel*. His entire life had been spent waiting for the Messiah so that he could rise and go up to Jerusalem; and in the end his soul departed on that longed for journey, but his body remained in the Diaspora.

Reception

Ish Hassid Haya was staged before audiences totalling over quarter of a million – about one eighth of the entire Jewish population of Israel at the time. Its financial success was impressive. The majority of theatre-goers during those years were of western origin.[31] The proportion of oriental to western Jews at the time[32] supports the estimate that a quarter or more of the entire *Ashkenazi* population of the country watched the play.[33] Many spectators also saw it more than once. There were innumerable journalists' reports and two records were produced – thus spreading its message to even wider audiences.

The critics "read" the play as a text bearing ideological significance – such as "reflecting" changes in the "structure of feeling" as well as a cultural experiment that indicated new directions. Some critics praised and others condemned, but none remained indifferent to the discussion that the play initiated on the Judaism of the Israeli Jew. Emil Feuerstein, critic for a religious journal, was convinced that an audience "held in the grip of longing for its own substance" was given "national satisfaction" by the play.[34] Moshe Shamir, whose approach was right-wing following the Six Day War, noted that the play was "not only an evening of entertainment, but perhaps also a sign of yearning for some sort of deep-rooted Jewishness."[35] In contrast, the "left-wing" and "centre" newspapers displayed a more critical reaction. Yoram Kaniuk objected to both the contents and structure of the play:

> I am not a believing man. But I shudder when I see a man who does not believe, who is not prepared for a true religious experience, suddenly fall upon the halo of a religious ceremony. Because we currently live in a time in which people have discovered religion anew, but do not understand that they are discovering only that part which is comfortable for them, and by embracing one part or another of the religion they are making fools of themselves [...] there is something repugnant or absurd in displaying Hassidism as a sort of army entertainment troupe.[36]

Ruth Hazan attacked the play and its message from the left-wing perspective of the Israeli political map, reading it as an unwanted result of

---

[31] Elihu Katz and Michael Gurevitch, *Leisure Culture in Israel: Types of Entertainment and Cultural Need*, Tel Aviv, Am Oved, 1973, 95–96, 102, 117, 120. (Hebrew)

[32] The total Jewish population of Israel at the end of 1968 was 2,434,800. At the end of 1967 the ethnic division was as follows: 48% oriental Jews and 52% Jews of western origin. Gad Levy, *Know Israel*, Jerusalem, Ministry of Education and Culture, 1971, 19. (Hebrew)

[33] Dan Almagor remembers most of the audience as being *Askenazi* and relatively elderly. Shlomo Nizan recalls places ("such as Kiryat Malachi", most of the population of which is of oriental origin) in which the play "had difficulty taking off".

[34] Emil Feuerstein, "*Ish Hassid Haya* at Habima", *Ha'Zofeh*, 18 October, 1968. (Hebrew)

[35] Moshe Shamir, "The Beautiful, the Ugly and the Confused", *Ma'ariv*, 17 March 1972. (Hebrew)

[36] Yoram Kaniuk, note 1.

the Six Day War:

> [...] The chauvinism, self-aggrandizement and self-congratulation that
> spread through the country [...] are neither to the benefit of the Jewish
> township nor to art, nor to the State. Nor is the dramatic feeling that we
> are all seated, every group of society, in the same boat facing a sea of
> hatred that could sink us at any moment [...] it is of course possible
> to say: why all this whining criticism about the audience enjoying itself
> [...] what exactly is the audience enjoying? The artistic quality? The
> profound contents? The language? Or themselves? In other words that
> wonderful nation that is always victorious. Always guards the embers.
> Always emigrates to Israel! A simply mighty nation![37]

The great success and the many subsequent "secondary texts"
(in the printed and electronic media), show that *Ish Hassid Haya* was no
ordinary play but a ritual for a particular group of the Jewish population.
The "horizon of expectations"[38] of the "community of spectators"[39] was
with/without the play focused on a shift and revision of attitude to
Jewish tradition. The play was not an isolated cultural phenomenon; its
intertextuality reveals it as a ritual of the new civil religion which,
according to Charles S. Liebman and Eliezer Don-Yehiya, had gained
a prominent position in Israeli culture following the Six Day War:

> Its goal was to unite and integrate the society around its conception of
> the Jewish tradition and the Jewish people; it no longer sought the
> creation of a new Jew and a new Jewish society [...] This is the *most
> ethnocentric* [my emphasis, D.U.] of all civil religions. It affirms all
> Jewish history and culture and gives special emphasis to the isolation of
> Jews and the hostility of Gentiles [...] a civil religion especially well suited
> to masses who are familiar with and attached to traditional symbols but
> unsophisticated concerning their explicit meaning.[40]

Dan Almagor credits the play with far-reaching effects, considering that
its "Story Theatre" style and structure influenced many subsequent
plays. From the point of view of Israeli musical culture, *Ish Hassid Haya*

---

[37] Ruth Hazan, "The Jewish *Shtetl* and Us", *Al Ha'Mishmar, Hotam*, 20 November, 1968.
(Hebrew)
[38] Susan Bennett, *Theatre Audiences: A Theory of Production and Reception*, London and New
York, Routledge, 1990, 51–55.
[39] Marvin Carlson, "Theatre Audiences and the Reading of Performance", *Theatre Semiotics:
Signs of Life*, Bloomington & Indianapolis, Indiana University Press, 1990, 13.
[40] Charles S. Liebman and Eliezer Don-Yehiya, "The Dilemma of Reconciling Tradition,
Culture and Political Needs: Civil Religion in Israel", *Religion and Politics in Israel*,
Bloomington, Indiana University Press, 1984, 53.

put Hassidic melodies on the cultural map, to the extent that they even acquired their own annual song festival. From the 1970s two of the playmakers, Yossi Yzraely and Shlomo Nizan, turned Jewish materials (mainly stories by Agnon and tales of Rabbi Nahman of Braslav) into a source for their work in the theatre. The political effect of the play is still bothering its creators in the 1990s, and attests to the acute secular-religious schism in Israel. Dan Almagor considers that "one should examine to what extent 'Rabbi Gedalia the tar-spreader' and 'Avram'le Melamed' influenced the increase in secular Jews returning to the ultra-Orthodox fold; as well as the proliferation of *uparatzta uparatzta* [one of the Gush Emunim anthems] circles." Shlomo Nizan, who still reveals a great fondness for the show's songs, can no longer sing them on stage for fear that "they'll say he's converted to ultra-Orthodoxy," and what is more: "if I had known that *Ish Hassid Haya* would lead to a great wave of 'Hassidism', I'm not sure I would have taken part in its production."

3
FEMINIST THEATRICAL CRITICISM OF JUDAISM

The story of the life of Bruria during the time of the Roman conquest (2nd century C.E.) – the only woman whose opinions on *halacha* [Jewish religious law] are mentioned in the Talmudic literature [the *halachic* literature of the 3rd to 6th centuries C.E.] – has been adapted in novel form in both Hebrew and other languages. The theatrical production of *Bruria* constitutes our "study case" in relating to the attitude of women's theatre in Israel toward the male-oriented Jewish tradition. Like the story of any woman, *Bruria* is about "the daughter of ..., the wife of ..."; except that the continuation is different, and the end is tragic, similar to the fate of many of those figures whose special status enhances the agony of their downfall.

Bruria has been performed by a group of Jerusalem actresses since 1982, and is a contemporary theatrical version of the story of the only woman mentioned in the sources as having studied the Torah and ruled on Jewish law. This highest form of activity in Judaism has traditionally been preserved for men alone, to the extent of creating an oxymoron of the notion of a woman studying or ruling on *halachic* law.

This chapter begins by examining the background of the fringe position of women's theatre within the Israeli theatrical system, before going on to present the various views of the life of Bruria as displayed by the Talmud, the Midrash [laws and legends studied from the Bible] and by Rashi [Rabbi Shlomo Yizhaki, an important 11th century French commentator on the Talmud], followed by a discussion of the central issue of the play itself.

Women in Israeli Theatre

The Hebrew theatre has been perceived by its audiences since its inception in the 1920s as a highbrow cultural activity whose contents are given great importance, to the extent of arousing public controversy following certain of its productions. Its audiences generally comprise the well-educated, who often deliberately choose original plays in order to examine for themselves, in a public place, and within their own "social group" the problems and conflicts which disturb them, including those questions of cultural identity which so bother an immigrant society. This combination of elements explains the importance of the public discussion of various issues in the Israeli theatre. In connection to the Israeli women's theatre, it is important to note the absence of certain subjects and "voices" from the plays.[1]

Among the "participants" in the Israeli social debate, as characterised by Yona Hadari-Ramage, the following are almost entirely absent: women, oriental Jews, and Palestinians:

> In the arena of "public thought", the Israeli discourse is generally one of men among themselves. A discourse of warriors, of fathers and sons, of buddies and even of rivals, etc. In the main the discourse is still that of the pioneering *Askenazi* Jew [of European origin], the white, blond, pure-in-deed male [...] his acts and words [...] they have suppressed all the others, religious, Asian and African immigrants, and women.[2]

Most of the Israeli theatre repertoire is a dialogue of male playwrights. The female characters have been depicted in the main from a male point of view. From the early period of settlement, before the establishment of the State, men were presented as those who made the desert bloom, who provided a defence against the marauding Arabs. Women's roles were restricted to mother-wife-sister-daughter figures: they were lovers, cooks, laundresses – but only rarely "allowed" to help on the land, perceived at that time as holy work.[3] During the time of the dispute with the Arabs it was the men who left to fight and the women who remained at home with the children. They were reserved the role of encouraging the son or husband to carry out his pioneering or security missions. This too was the role of women in plays about the War of Independence (1947–1949) – the woman who takes part in the battle (not as a fighter) provides a "mirror" for the heroism of the man. One such woman, Shosh, in the play *The Desert Plains of the Negev* by Yigal Mossinsohn (1949),

---

[1] Pierre Macherey (1966) claims that "What is important in the work is what it does not say", *Pour une théorie de la production littéraire*, Paris, Maspero, 1971, 105–10.

[2] Yona Hadari-Ramage, *Thinking It Over: Conflicts in Israeli Public Thought*, Ramat Efal, Yad Tabenkin and Yediot Aharonot, 1994, 20. (Hebrew)

[3] The playwright Esther Izbitsky relates to this situation in her play, which she also directed, *Pioneering Women Settle on Gravel*, about the beginnings of Zionist settlement in Israel:
"There was a battle for equality. The female members of Hashomer [a Jewish guard organization in Israel from 1909–1920] rebelled over the right to actively participate in guard duties, and over equal social rights. In Hashomer the women worked in the kitchen and other services. In the early days of the kibbutz there was equality, but not without sly tricks, [...] it is documented that they let a female member plough with a pair of oxen; despite everyone knowing that you can't use them to plough [...] at Tel Chai there was a bitter struggle between the male and female members over the right to carry a gun." Emanuel Bar-Kedma, "What's That Work to Us", *Yediot Aharonot*, 24 April 1981. (Hebrew)

serves as a self-effacing voice justifying the rough behaviour of the male Hebrew warrior:

> [...] and try and tell me that you don't want to kill, that you don't want war, you don't want to murder poor *fellahin* [Arab peasants] from the Land of Israel or Egypt – but you must – and then we end up showing off, using *ahalan* and *kef* and *mabsut* [Arabic terms for 'welcome', 'great fun' and 'I'm fine'] – we don't want to sink so far that we see the open abyss, – for Uzi and Uri [Hebrew male names] have become young killers of men before they have even stroked the plait on a young girl's head.[4]

In plays from the period following the establishment of the State, women in many cases present the changing values in Israeli society. They are blamed for the disintegrating pioneering ideal and the hedonism and selfishness that have negatively influenced the world of the male, who had formerly devoted all his energy to the Zionist enterprise. It is partic-ularly interesting to note that from the beginning of the 1970s, female characters in the plays of Hanoch Levin, the most successful of Israeli playwrights, constitute a sort of caricature of the Jewish mother, depicted as a domineering, graspingly materialistic monster.[5]

The Hebrew theatre has only a small number of women play-wrights. The number of original plays written by women that reach the stage is low, and this has remained the case even in the 1980s and 1990s, despite an increase in the number of playwrights. The male playwright domination of Israeli theatre is only one of its masculine characteristics. Administrative positions (artistic and otherwise) in the large theatres were always reserved for men. There are a few women who have admin-istered or are currently administering small theatres, but only two in the entire history of the Hebrew theatre have managed the 'intermediate' theatres (Ada Ben-Nahum [deceased] and Zippi Pines). At first glance, it would appear that Israeli theatre has reserved an important place for its actresses. However, their status as stage figures is determined by texts written and directed by men. A female character is frequently a "mirror" for the male characters, as in *The Desert Plains of the Negev*, in which Zvi demonstrates a typical reaction to Shosh's comments: "Let's not talk about it any more [...] give me your hand, Shosh, I always did say you were 'cute', 'That's it'".[6]

---

[4] Yigal Mossinsohn, *In the Desert Plains of the Negev*, Tel Aviv, Or-Am, 1989, 20. (Hebrew)
[5] Similar examples can also be found in other plays, such as *A Simple Story* by S.Y. Agnon (1979), adapted for theatre by Yossi Yzraely, as well as plays by Aharon Megged and Edna Maziah. see: Shosh Weitz, "A Screen in Your Eyes", *Nogah*, 13, winter 1987, 20. (Hebrew)
[6] Mossinsohn, note 4, 20.

Under such conditions it is "natural" for women's theatre in Israel to find its place on the fringes. The repertoire of women's plays dealing with women's issues is surprisingly small. It contains theatrical texts presenting the "authentic" views of women on events involving men, such as a women's conversation about war; or the "social" plays which deal with family violence or battered women, etc. The number of plays aimed at "re-writing" the place of women in Jewish and Israeli myths is particularly small. Two of these predate *Bruria* and were staged in 1981: *Woman from the Land* by Yael Feyler and *Pioneering Women Settle on Gravel* by Esther Izbitsky. Both plays examine male myths from a feminist viewpoint. *Woman from the Land* (staged at the Akko Fringe Theatre festival) is the tale of Lilith, the first woman, according to the Jewish legend, to be created from the earth. It comprises verses, stories and sayings from the Jewish tradition. Lilith, according to legend from the time of the *gaonim* [*yeshiva* heads in Babylon and Israel from the 6th century onwards], was God's first experiment at creating a partner for the first man. She was a stubborn woman who would not agree to lie beneath Adam, nor was she ready to relinquish her equal rights; there was thus no choice but to create Eve. Lilith, however, continued to rampage through the world, giving birth to small demons. Yael Feyler felt an empathy for the character of Lilith:

> I felt that she could express me. And what I wanted was to say something as a woman – a changing, deliberating woman, about my life, my nature, about other women. By means of the theatre [...] and really the path taken by "the woman" in the play, is the way in which I appear to have moved from the first Lilith – through suppression and punishment, to Eve, within whom conflicting forces are at work: she seeks Lilith but is still wary of her. She learns from her but is cautious about following her blindly.[7]

Pioneering Women Settle on Gravel by Esther Izbitsky (only performed five times on Stage 2 of the Haifa Municipal Theatre), examines the myth of the revolution of Zionism from the viewpoint of its female participants: women who do not appear in the stories of the Zionist *aliyah rishonah* [first wave of Jewish immigration, 1882–1903] other than in passive or silent roles. One such figure is "a sort of quiet, diligent nun, free of anger, a figure lacking in any antagonism towards male society."[8] As an antithesis to this image, the playwright-director instructed her actresses to display ceaseless activity: from raking gravel to kneading dough – hard, demanding physical tasks that reflect the hard, thankless

---

[7] Yael Feiler, "In the Footsteps of Lilith", *Nogah*, 4, 1982, 28. (Hebrew)
[8] Nurit Kahana, "Pioneering Women Settle on Gravel", *Nogah*, 3, 1981, 34. (Hebrew)

labour of these anonymous women who live in the shadow of their men. The men are represented in the play by metal poles featuring plywood heads displaying the countenances of central figures of the time, such as Theodor Herzl, the founder of Zionism and visionary of a Jewish State, or Chaim Brenner, an important writer from the period of settlement. This kind of caricature expresses the women's anger towards the male-oriented history of the early settlement period. The play is a collage from the period, and incorporates such phrases as that of Herzl:

> Do not turn our darling girls into warriors demanding to fight. Let them wander in the vineyards, pick lilies and carnations and braid them in their hair. Let the young girls continue to blossom hidden from the eyes of men, like paintings veiled by a scarf.

The affiliation of women's theatre to the fringes of the system is particularly apparent in its specific forms. The repertory theatre trends toward works of a coherent nature; narratives with a beginning, middle and end, as well as a tendency to the spectacular: technologically advanced stages, sophisticated scenery, varied lighting, and a wide selection of costume and props. The identity of the women's theatre has developed from its objection to the central, patriarchal mainstream, and its consequent choice of alternative characteristics. Both fringe theatre and women's theatre trend towards the fragmentary and minimalist. Such characteristics are particularly suitable to emphasize their message and contradict those views and beliefs which differ from the "accepted". In works by the Theatre Company of Jerusalem (TCJ), especially *Bruria*, the theatrical-experimental form serves the demand for "a new Judaism" – a Judaism in which there is a well-deserved place for women, who choose for this purpose – following the path of the American intellectual writer Cynthia Ozick – to set out against the injustice inherent in the sub-human status demonstrated by the Torah toward women:

> If we look only into Torah, we see that the ubiquitousness of women's condition applies here as well. [...] Women's quality of lesserness, of otherness, is laid down at the very beginning, as paradigm and as rule: at the start of the Creation of the World women is given an inferior place.[9]

The masculine model of theatre is presented in one of the TCJ's plays, *The Last Play* (1992), as a model to be shaken off; it echoes the words of the French poet, playwright and essayist, Hélène Cixous. Cixous, who is not known by the TCJ, closely approaches them in her

---

[9] Cynthia Ozick, "Notes toward Finding the Right Question", *Forum*, 35, 1979, 56.

concepts and plays, and will be helpful in understanding their theatrical activity. In a short essay "Aller à la mer",[10] Cixous refers to the problematic link between women and theatre. The theatre serves the "male fantasy" in which well-known female figures (such as Electra, Ophelia or Cordelia) are always the victims, always exploited, disappointed, and serve as a mirror for the heroic male. Such a theatre suppresses femininity which refuses to remain silent: "and if, like Cordelia, she finds the strength to assert a femininity which refuses to be the mirror of her father's ravings, she will die."[11]

The Last Play, a collaborative work by Joyce (Rinat) Miller and Aliza Elion-Israeli, offers a re-write ("writing as re-enactment" from the masculine model according to Hélène Cixous) of feminine characters:

> So he gave me the stage as if it belonged to him […] he wants a mono-drama? Monodrama? He probably thinks that I'll begin with a major classic role. Medea (acting:) "We women are a cursed race." That's what Euripides put in her mouth before he let her kill her two children. Why do I need to be a party to this perversion written by men? Why do I constantly continue doing exactly what Michel wants, even now, on the stage that is all mine, when there is nobody here to bother me with their Doll's House fantasies. Michel wanted me to play Medea like a witch and Ophelia like a betrayed and innocent virgin […] What's he afraid of? I've actually played both of them as clever women with great sensitivity, standing on the brink of an abyss. How I love acting. I already have inside me a collection of tragic women, witches, seductresses, creations of the male imagination that I enjoy passing through me.

The TCJ has several features in common with other women's theatre: its organisation, themes and theatrical forms and strategies. From the organisational point of view, this theatre has no hierarchy: its female participants share their ideas, the writing, acting and directing. They are assisted by guest directors and additional actors/actresses. They work as an ensemble, with most of the writing done by Aliza Elion-Israeli. Preparation is accompanied by research by all the participants, and does not cease with the first performance. Their choices involve the audience, and they are known for their tendency to continue shaping the play even after its preparations are "complete" (as in *Sarah Take 1* which was changed and updated to *Sarah Take 2*). This continuous process leads to an extensive examination throughout the life of the play, of questions relating to feminist issues.[12] There is thus a particular significance in

---

[10] This title can be translated as "Going to the Seaside" or "Going to the Mother".

[11] Hélène Cixous, "Aller à la mer", *Le Monde*, 28 Avril 1977, trans. Barbara Kerslake in *Modern Drama*, Vol. 27, No. 4, December 1984, 546–8.

[12] Elaine Aston, *An Introduction to Feminism and Theatre*, London and New York, Routledge, 1995, 62.

regard to *Bruria*, which has been staged since 1982 in various versions: in Hebrew, English, and even as a monodrama. The playwright and actresses use various techniques of persuasion, such as different theatrical styles: comedy, musical or cabaret.[13] Among the accepted distinctions between the different directions of women's theatre – "bourgeois" feminism, radical and "socialist/materialist" – the TCJ tends towards the radical which proposes a feminist counter-culture. This direction is characterized by Elaine Aston as "investigating the possibilities of a gender based ritualized style of theatre which seeks the emotional, mythical and historical keys to woman centred culture."[14]

The TCJ – "A Jewish-Israeli Female Voice"

The Jerusalem Theatre Group has been active since 1982 "mainly with plays from Jewish sources". Its Jewish identity is linked with the biography of each of its participants. Gabriella Lev, Ruth Wieder and Aliza Elion-Israeli refer to the Jewish tradition in both their work and lives. Gabriella and Ruth are sisters who grew up in Australia in a religious family of holocaust survivors, while Aliza was born and raised in a secular Israeli home. They keep many of the *mitzvot* [religious commandments] "but the concept 'religious' means little to me" states Elion-Israeli. In the town of Yerucham, among Jews of Moroccan origin, she encountered a use of the Hebrew language that reflected its ancient origins: "and then I understand that it is impossible to create Hebrew theatre without referring to the Hebrew myths." For Ruth "working with the Jewish sources was already taken for granted from the initial stage of preparing *Bruria*," while for Aliza "there were still difficulties" and she was sure that "it is no coincidence that the group began with one Israeli and two new immigrants. It would have been impossible to carry this out with Israeli actresses alone."

In contemporary feminist theatre in which women seek to present an "active subject", they turn towards an "interrogative style" of text and performance practice,[15] demonstrated by the work of the TCJ as described by Aliza Elion-Israeli: "our process evolved from within the tradition [...] study as a way of life [...] the creative system is therefore a process of study. Study means the word, and study is the oral tradition of Torah. We thus approach the material as it has been taught in the *havrutot* [groups of students] throughout the years in the *yeshivot* [colleges for Torah study]".

---

[13] Such as, *My Sister-in-Law and I*, 1992, The Jerusalem Theatre Company, which is "a funny, touching play with music and songs, about the daily lives of women."
[14] Aston, note 12, 68.
[15] Lizbeth Goodman, *Contemporary Feminist Theatres: To Each Her Own*, London and New York, Routledge, 1993, 21; Aston, note 12, 38.

"Re-writing" of theatre history characterises the feminist discussion in the theatre and is an attempt to explain the absence of women from theatre histories, as well as an attempt to uncover those women playwrights whose works did not achieve documentary status. A similar approach can be found among the TCJ. Gabriella Lev begins her history of the theatre with a Judaism which, according to her version – incorporated women:

> The Jews were the first to make theatre. A theatre of the synagogue and temple. At that time the women would sit at the back and sing. But Judaism in the Midrash took away the women's voice ("the voice of a woman is a nakedness"), which constitutes power, and made her silent. We, by our theatrical activity, are saying: the woman is there, she exists and has a voice. We seek the way to return the women their voice.[16]

Burdening the women with dumbness is also described by Hélène Cixous. In one of her references to her own Jewishness (which she terms *juifemme* – *Jewoman*) she explains the subordination of the *juifemme* as an arbitrary act by a male whose claims to the superiority of a father as God, she refutes:

> What is a father? The one taken for father. The one recognised as the true one. "Truth", the essence of fatherhood, its force as law. The "chosen" father.[17]

Cixous believes that the main political and ethical roles of the theatre lie in its correcting injustice and rehabilitating disabilities, as well as in creating an unbiased openness to the "Other" (*ibid.* 127–144). There is a clear trend in the Jerusalem Theatre Group repertoire towards those "Other(s)" in Israeli society: women, oriental Jews, and Arabs.[18]

An additional similarity between Cixous' theories and practice and those of the Jerusalem actresses lies in their emphasis on the importance of *voice*. A woman's voice is that which had sounded in song from time immemorial, before the ruling that banished it and restricted it to plays written in the authoritative male language of the schism. For Cixous, a vocal statement is preferable due to its proximity to song, and

---

[16] Lee Evron, "Blessed Be He For Making Me a Woman", *Jerusalem*, 29 October 1993. (Hebrew)

[17] Hélène Cixous et Cathérine Clément, *La Jeune Née*, "Sorties", Paris, Union Générale d'Editions, 10/18, 1975, 191. Taken from the English translation, Hélène Cixous and Cathérine Clément, *The Newly Born Woman*, trans. Betsy Wing, Minneapolis, University of Minnesota Press, 1991, 103.

[18] *Even the Birds*, 1988, by Aliza Elion-Israeli and in *The Jasmin Bush*, 1995, by Elion-Israeli and Ali Kleiboh.

thus as a means of expression for the subconscious. She tends to prefer the associative nature of music and has reservations regarding the linearity of philosophical and literary discourse, which she identifies with logocentrism – and "couples" with phallocentrism.[19] The TCJ actresses study the theatrical uses of voice as a principal means of expression in their work and, according to Aliza Elion-Israeli, "work hard on the connection between language, voice and body movements – a connection that appears to us to be of particular importance in Hebrew." Gabriella Lev adds:

> With *Bruria* we began work on the voice in the style of the Roy Hart Theatre, which visited here during one of the Israel Festivals. It is a use of voice, not of language, and it incorporates everything that the human voice is capable of producing. We developed this work structure, following a great deal of observation of *hazzanut* [prayer accompanied by song and melody] and oriental influence, and work on Hebrew and Aramaic melodies.[20]

The Company Repertoire

The 1975 production of *Women for Women* was one of the first to present "the female experience" on the Israeli stage. The play maintained a direct link with its audience and demanded their participation; a novel approach for the period. Elion-Israeli notes that this was not "a militant decision to create women's theatre; but if a group of women gather together the subject naturally turns to women. It is highly typical for beginning artists to make use of autobiographical material and of those issues that concern them." Such beginnings influence the continuation: "Our theatre," continues Elion-Israeli, "is part of our life. What we stage belongs to a particular chapter in our lives." Their second play, *Soft People* (1976), featured innovations in the use of large puppets and the introduction of three themes which recur in all their plays: "the subjects of Judaism, femininity and the holocaust."

    Bruria is the first play by the company to examine a tale from the ancient sources. This too reveals an interesting similarity to Cixous, who examined the myths as means and case studies to disclose their suppressed femininity, in order to question the male dominance in these stories.[21] The director Joyce Miller, who was involved in the early 1980s with

---

[19] Cixous, note 17, 119.

[20] Naomi Gal, "As if it is Something Strange about Women", *Modern Times, Yediot Aharonot Suppl.*, 6 December 1990. (Hebrew)

[21] In her historical plays Cixous uses theatrical space "as a framework for the mythic narratives she wishes to develop." Morag Shiach, *Hélène Cixous: A Politics of Writing*, London and New York, Routledge, 1991, 106.

"ancient myths", encountered Hebrew myths through the JTC. "We supplied her with totally amorphous material [...] [and] she succeeded in 'translating' it into western theatre." Since *Bruria*, the JTC repertoire has dealt in the main with "disclosing the lost women" in Jewish tradition by means of plays about famous figures (such as Sarah and Esther) as well as anonymous women who appear in the literature of the Palestinian and Babylonian Talmud.[22]

An important part of Cixous' theoretical and practical work relates to *deconstruction*: "Derridean deconstruction will have been the greatest ethical critical warning gesture of our time: careful! Let us not be the dupe of logocentric authority."[23] Deconstruction serves her as a strategy in demolishing those myths which support the patriarchal system and in abrogating their "natural" status. She conceives the *Oresteia* as a narrative in which patriarchism overcomes and defeats matriarchism, and firmly installs father and son, Agamemnon and Orestes, at the centre of things; while the daughter, Electra, serves the aims of phallocentrism, for her voice is the clearest in its demand to revenge her father's death by killing her mother.[24] The JTC too studies, dissects and rewrites the myths from their feminist aspect. Their approach to the figure of Sarah is similar to Cixous' feminist "reading" of myths, according to Elion-Israeli:

> One can approach the sources from contradictory directions. As in the case of Sarah. One can claim: How does one turn the mother of the nation into a barren woman? And not just barren, but without a womb? What sort of culture are we? In which a woman who is supposed to be the 'fertile mother', has her tale told by a male culture; which removes her womb so that she will not be able to give birth naturally but only by means of a miracle from God – who is a man. The image of Sarah in particular is important because historically she is situated on the border between the matriarchal and the patriarchal cultures. This does indeed generate anger. But that's the way it is, that's the tradition we have for Sarah. Sarah does not speak out in any of the Bible stories. She is a silent character. We do not set out against what is told. We understand it in our own way. For us, Sarah is the hero of the play. She speaks throughout the play and we give her many opportunities to say what we think she says; mainly to say the world of Abraham her husband is not her world. She says to her son Isaac: "The world that you and your father have created is not my world [...] my world is a world of plenty [...] of embryos and of benediction."

An all-encompassing viewpoint directs the JTC repertoire and its interest in relationships between the sexes. This can be illustrated with

---

[22] In the plays: *One Thousand Esthers and Hester*, 1985, *Bed and Deaths*, 1990, *Sarah*, 1993.

[23] Hélène Cixous, "Preface", *The Hélène Cixous Reader*, Edited by Susan Sellers, London and New York, Routledge, 1994, xviii.

[24] Cixous, note 16, 191–8.

the aid of Cixous's list of hierarchical contrasts that shaped western thought. Cixous refers to such contrasts as "Parole/Ecriture", "Matter/Form", "Head/Heart", "Culture/Nature", and particularly the contrast between man and woman. Each pair demonstrates a relationship of suppression among its components; and each pair is trapped within a violent conflict. Without nature, culture is meaningless, yet despite this, culture struggles to negate nature. In a patriarchal society the "man/women" contrast turns the woman into the "Other" – vital to reinforcing self-awareness of the superior male identity. However, the dependence on the "Other" also poses a constant threat to the man and intensifies his need to suppress. Sexual differences serve a method of force in which difference, or "Otherness", is tolerated only when it is suppressed. As in the famous fairy tale of the Sleeping Beauty, the woman is presented as asleep, until the man kisses her; and only his kiss can lend her reality, within which she is immediately subordinated to the desires of "the prince". (*ibid.* 115–20)

French feminism, principally Cixous, presents the male/female dualism as deterministic and does not believe in a harmonious solution. The JTC raises both questions and doubts in this direction. One of the plays staged by the company, *Elef Esther ve'Hester* [*A Thousand Esthers and Hester*] [Hester is a play on the Hebrew word "to hide" together with the name of Queen Esther] (1985), suggests an interpretation of the *Book of Esther* as a text of "unity of opposites" – cosmic opposites of good and bad which only a woman succeeds in settling and thus preventing a holocaust. "In our interpretation of *The Book of Esther*," states Elion-Israeli, "we showed that suppressing feminist power is a proven recipe for creating a holocaust. Esther thus demands of the editors of the Bible: 'let it be written down for the generations that I prevented a holocaust'." And while *Bruria*, as understood by its director Joyce Miller, "is anchored in duality", she finds difficulty in seeing a possibility of settling the opposing sides and appears to restrict herself to placing them side by side as an ontological basis for human reality, in which there is an ongoing struggle of different forces, mainly male/female:

> Two actresses, two bowls, two sheets of fabric, two colours on the fabric [...] actresses with contrasting natures using contrasting styles [...] *the question to which we have not tried to provide an explicit answer is whether such duality really can be solved by unequivocal unification.*[25]

The "duality" of *Bruria* is recognizable in its feminist narrative structure that sharply diverges from the masculine narrative characteristic

---

[25] Rinat Joyce Miller, "Notes on Directing *Maaseh Bruria*", *Bamah*, 94, 1983, 11–20. (Hebrew)

of mainstream theatre. Teresa De Laurtis, in her semiotic research into cinema, characterises narrative strategies according to gender, most of which fall into the masculine category. Between the genders, on screen (and on stage) there is a rigid division of labour: the man in many narratives is the subject who initiates the path to adventure, while the woman (the "princess") is merely the sought after object, neither active nor activating.[26] To contest this dominant model, Cixous proposes a theatre with a powerful physical female presence at its centre. Non-theatrical. Without a barrier between stage and auditorium. And there is "no need for plot or action."[27] Like Cixous (and Teresa De Laurtis), Gabriella Lev reveals a concept of separation between the male and female models:

> The model of western theatre – a linear plot constructed towards a climax followed by relaxation of tension – is a masculine model. Our plays are constructed along feminist lines: they are episodic, circular, containing various interwoven elements, all equally important. We leave things open, which also contrasts with the masculine model.[28]

The Legend of Bruria

"The Legend of Bruria" is the tale of the daughter of Rabbi Hanina ben Tradyon and the wife of Rabbi Meir. As mentioned earlier, Bruria is the only woman whose opinions on Jewish law were mentioned in Talmudic literature and accepted by the learned rabbinical authorities of her generation.[29] Thus, her image provides an almost total contradiction to the male spirit of the *halachic* literature, as noted by Shulamit Valler:

> The literature of our learned forefathers, in all its genres, is a literature written according to a male viewpoint, which perceives the female sex as a weak sex, for which nature has destined functions and purposes different to those intended for men […] This is a literature written by a powerful group, dominant and active, which revealed a consideration for the other group, but nonetheless caused it to become passive and dependent, and prevented its participation in social and spiritual life.[30]

---

[26] "The mythical subject is constructed as human being and as male; he is the active principle of culture, the establisher of distinction, the creator of differences. Female is what is not susceptible to transformation, to life or death; she (it) is an element of plot-space, a topos, a resistance, matrix and matter." Teresa De Laurtis, *Alice Doesn't: Feminism, Semiotics, Cinema*, Bloomington, Indiana University Press, 1984, 119.

[27] Cixous, note 11, 547.

[28] Lee Evron, note 16.

[29] *Tosefta Kelim, Baba Qamma* 4:17; and, *Tosefta Kelim, Baba Metzia* 1:6.

[30] Shulamith Valler, *Women and Womanhood in the Stories of the Babylonian Talmud*, Tel Aviv, Ha'Kibbutz Ha'Meuchad, 1993, 12. (Hebrew)

The tale of Bruria is not a continuous "story" about the life of this woman, but nine episodes fragments scattered throughout the Talmud and the Midrash. Were it not for its horrifying end, as told by Rashi, it would not have aroused so great an interest for protest groups and for interpretation by women's theatre. Daniel Boyarin terms the collection of pieces that relate to Bruria in the Talmud and Midrash as the "cultural fantasy" of rabbis, whose real interest lies in the "acknowledgement/denial" of the possibility of women studying the Torah.[31]

It is Bruria's end that shapes her "story". Traditional sources devoted to her personality and achievements begin the tale of Bruria with her family – her parents and her brother, who died a violent death; her marriage to Rabbi Meir; examples of her legal capabilities and her aggressive/resolute character (such as the story of the student whom she kicked); the tale of the death of both her sons; the tale of her sister forced into prostitution by the Romans and saved by Rabbi Meir; and finally, Bruria's succumbing to seduction by one of Rabbi Meir's students – a seduction instigated by Rabbi Meir; the story of Bruria's suicide and the shamed Rabbi Meir's departure to the Diaspora. It is not known exactly when the story of Bruria's end was created; whether during the period of the Talmud, or prior to Rashi in the 11th century. In any event, Rashi tells the story as taken for granted. It is important that although the various versions of Bruria's story began in the period of the Talmud and continued until the early Middle Ages, in the 20th century, too, traditional sources continue to tell the tale, encountering no difficulty whatsoever with its ending.[32] For contemporary commentators, the "natural" acceptance of Bruria's end has turned it into a cultural paradigm of the attitude of Judaism to women. The writer Cynthia Ozick is one of its readers to "disclose" the male logic behind the shameful end to Bruria's life story:

> The famously brilliant Bruria, celebrated not only as wife of Rabbi Meir, but also in her own right, was known to speak satirically of those rabbinic passages which make light of the intellect of women. To punish her for her impudence, a rabbinic storyteller, bent on mischief toward intellectual women, reinvented Bruria as seductress. She comes down to us twice notorious: first as a kind of bluestocking, again as a licentious woman. There is no doubt that we are meant to see a connection between the two.[33]

---

[31] Daniel Boyarin, *Carnal Israel: Reading Sex in Talmudic Culture*, Berkeley, University of California Press, 1993, 182.
[32] As in *Otzar Israel*, Jerusalem, Pardess, 1952, 191; *Toldot Tanaim ve'Amoraim*, by Rabbi Aharon Heyman, Jerusalem, Kiria Ne'emana, 1954, Vol. 1, 295; see also: Naftali Krauss, "A Big Woman whose Name is Bruria", *Ma'ariv*, 11 March 1983. (Hebrew)
[33] Ozick, note 9, 43–4.

It is no coincidence that when Elion-Israeli tells the tale of Bruria, she begins from the end, and makes no secret of the insult to her as a Jewish woman:

> *Bruria* tells about the life of Bruria who was wife of Rabbi Meir. Rabbi Meir was one of the greatest rabbis of his generation [...] and one of the boldest. He was so daring that he could say that 'impure' was 'pure' and 'pure' was 'impure' [...]. Rabbi Meir was very controversial. For he attempted to construct a moral ethics with both good and bad being one and the same. This is almost impossible. His wife was Bruria. His wife heard him once teach that "women are frivolous" and she argued with him about it. He replied that "On your life, you will end up admitting that they are right – you will see that the end of your life will prove this claim". And what did he do, this great rabbi: He sent one of his students to tempt her into evil. This is the story. I am telling you the story as it is. "The student importuned her for many days until she agreed. When the matter became known to her she strangled herself." Who was Bruria? She was a woman who taught at the *Beth Midrash* [place for Torah study]. Imagine her during that period, a woman teaching! They say that she could teach 300 *mishniot* [chapters of discussion in the *halacha*] a day by heart. A tremendous number. She could be seen today as the Dean of the Law Faculty. This was a quarrelling couple. And after the deed was done, Rabbi Meir fled to Babylon and died. The entire family of both these powerful intellectuals broke up. If you examine the Talmud you will discern that every story about Rabbi Meir and Bruria appears. to contain spelling mistakes. She is called 'he' and he is called 'she'. Relying on this story and on an entire year's study of the sources, we have constructed the play *Bruria*. The play is about Bruria. About this woman. About her family.

The idea of staging "the story of Bruria" presented itself to Gabriella Lev as a protest about her shameful death. Her sister Ruth Wieder joined her; as a *chozeret be-tshuva* [returnee to the religious fold] she too had found the gates of religious law still closed to women in the second half of the 20th century. This is thus the tale of two sisters from the Talmud presented by two actress sisters, condemning the sole "masculine" right to study the Torah and protesting the denigration of the female image to that of a sexual accessory. Lev recounts:

> One day I found out from Rabbi Menachem Fruman that Bruria appears in the Talmud in *Avoda Zara*. He took out his Talmud and showed me that in the commentaries by Rashi it is written that Bruria scorned those Talmudic scholars who said that women are frivolous. "On your life, you will end up admitting that they are right" (said Rabbi Meir) and directed one of his students to tempt her into evil. And the student importuned her for many days until she agreed. When the matter

became known to her she strangled herself. I felt something physical when I heard this story. I was so angry that I wanted to find out more about her [...] I discovered a sensual woman with a strong character.[34]

Performance of *Bruria*

At the beginning of their work on the play the actresses and director attempted various improvisations. Elion-Israeli describes the process:

We sat "like Bruria". We talked "like her". For there is a lot written about her in the sources. One day I said: "That's it. We aren't going to do psychological improvisations, seeking motivations, like Stanislavski. The stories are in the Talmud. The Talmud is an oral tradition. We shall learn the stories by heart". While studying them by heart we came to understand that it is impossible to simply take Bruria and turn her into a dithering housewife, or – by contrast, into a university professor in a dilemma. Because of the mythological nature of her image, and the beauty of the language, it is not possible to role play; we have to work using the format of a narrator; without going into the various psycho-logical questions that arise, and also without trying to build the play around them. We discovered a language that we are still continuing to investigate, and the play was written in the language of the sources, apart from the interlinking scenes in modern Hebrew that I introduced.

Lev adds that during the work "we reached the conclusion that the sources should not be altered because they were so powerful, and we decided to make them the main text of the play [...] although we still needed to find the theatrical 'shape' to suit the story."

Bruria is a play for two actresses, intended from the outset for a small auditorium at the Akko Festival of fringe theatre; for a theatre of minimalist means which emphasizes the work of the actresses, principally their voices. On a long narrow stage, "the actresses seek the past [...] in order to reveal the meaning of the present [...] and thus [...] the *mise en scène* [is] modern-ancient."[35] The actresses do not wear make-up and their clothing "is of the sort worn at any time", which could be seen as "rehearsal clothing" (*ibid.* 15). The basic costume and lack of make-up enable simple transitions from character to character throughout the course of the play. The narrators can in this manner "*play themselves at any moment*" [emphasis mine, D.U.] (*ibid.*). This is an important aspect of the play, for its three participants – the playwright and the two actresses – began their search "from a strong personal motivation – to

---

[34] Naomi Gal, note 20.
[35] Miller, note 25, 15.

discover in Bruria's life a meaning that touched their own lives as young women living in Israel" (*ibid.* 12).

The director Joyce Miller aimed at a style that would "suggest Japanese theatre to the audience" (*ibid.* 14). Such an approach expresses her wish to turn the "tool" – the form of the play – into the "message" (*ibid.* 11); a style that is restrained in theatrical signs, which serve different purposes according to the dramatic requirement,[36] such as gestures that assist in changing roles, and strips of fabric that indicate new identities and new situations. This limited exchange of signs is aimed at diverting attention from the "theatre" and focusing it instead on the tale that is being told and its meaning, which is a framework for a caustic Jewish – Israeli-Feminist statement.

The performance style "avoided a mystic emphasis" (*ibid.* 13), but nonetheless managed to "awaken associations instead of defining them" (*ibid.* 15). The need for a new interpretation guided the presentation of "another" reality and invited different strategies from those of the male narrative: "I make my statement from the 'feminist side' by means of an artistic form," states Gabriella Lev, "therefore we call upon the images and dreams of the spectator [...] we do not dictate interpretations [...] the images we use are 'dreamlike' and serve to awaken memories, but they must be exact in their purpose, their place and their reference to other images."[37] Thus, for example, Miller prefers a high stage so that the actresses can create the image of a row of inscriptions on stone "and the gestures of their hands clearly describe the shapes of the Hebrew letters."[38] The majority of movement in the performance is by the hands (at the expense of the arms and legs) and the main action is of "writing". The emphasis on writing and the act of re-writing the myth appear at the beginning of the play when the actresses write the names of the *dramatis personae* in pseudo-ancient Hebrew letters on the backcloth.

The story in the play is mainly supported by the actresses' voices. Elion-Israeli states: "A great deal of work was done on the internal writing of the text and the musicality of the language. The work was accompanied by a search for a basic sound/tone for each tale and for its ramifications." However, "despite the great importance of the words, the message is not a verbal one. The message belongs to the area that

---

[36] Jindrich Honzl's characterization of Japanese theatre matches Miller's aims: "The Japanese stage also uses spatial instruction for every means of theatrical expression [...] it is not necessary for space to be marked by space, sound by sound, light by means of light [...] what will happen in the theatre is that 'we shall see the voice'." Jindrich Honzl, "La mobilite du signe théâtral", *Travail Théâtral*, 4, 1971, 13.

[37] Evron, note 16.

[38] Miller, note 25, 13.

stimulates all the senses and the intellect." The vocal work of the actresses moves from the "tuneful" statements of Ruth Wieder to the somewhat declamatory spoken style of Gabriella Lev, incorporating all possibilities inbetween.

The play has three parts, featuring three different versions of the story, as noted by the director:

> In fact, the story is told to the audience three times: in the prologue; in scenes 1–7; and in the epilogue. Scenes 1–7 provide a dramatization and expand upon the summary given in the prologue – in fact they use the information already provided and present it graphically and verbally through an expanded repetition. The epilogue serves as a double mirror for both prologue and epilogue (*ibid.* 40)

None of the audience can thus escape at least one version of the story, particularly its bitter end, which is revealed only after expectations have been raised, towards the end of the play. The purpose of the prologue is to present the story as "a very masculine text", concise and linear.[39] This is followed by a feminist "re-written" expansion of the life of Bruria, climaxing in the epilogue which shatters the tale.

The *opening* constitutes a sort of lecture whose purpose, as explained by Lev, is "to set out all the historical facts before the spectator." This is a tale in which it is the men, such as Rabbi Meir, one of the greatest rabbis of the Talmud, and the rest of the male figures who are identified and given names, who are the active figures. As they are killed in the story, their names are struck out on the backcloth with imitation blood. This is a tale entirely comprised of action and "elimination" of characters, with logical continuity of plot. The only scene not incorporated is Rashi's story of Bruria's bitter end. The play states: "according to Rashi she committed suicide because of 'the deeds of Bruria'," and does not expand. The narrator declaims these words in a crescendo and spills all the red colour she is holding upon the paper.

"*This is the whole story. But what do you hear in it?*" (and this is not the whole story for its end is missing.) This question opens the feminist deconstruction of the male story. The two narrators are two sisters who enter into the images of Bruria and her sister, let down their hair and comb their hair, wash in clear water and dress in white. This is an intimate moment on the wedding day of Bruria and Rabbi Meir, in which all the characters in the story were still alive. The unmarried sister asks Bruria what marriage is; and she wonders at the significance of the relationship between Rabbi Meir and Bruria, both of whom "like two uprooted mountains stand facing one another. Will they grind down one

---

[39] Aliza Elion-Israeli, "Working on *Maaseh Bruria*", *Bamah*, 94, 1983, 21. (Hebrew)

another to the end, or will they have the grace to desist?" And Bruria replies: "Mercy will come from the Heavens."

Throughout the play there is no mercy "from the Heavens". The "structure" of organization of the tales in the second part is of action or inaction accompanied by reward or punishment. Mainly punishment! The penalties are burning, stoning, sudden death of children, prostitution and suicide, all of which are given persuasive explanations. Thus, in retrospect, the story of this family becomes a collection of events that illustrates the male judgement of Jewish law, which is presented from the feminist viewpoint as harsh, obdurate and cruel: Rabbi Hanina ben Tradyon, Bruria's father, was condemned to being burnt at the stake, his wife was condemned to death and Bruria's sister was condemned by the Romans to a life of prostitution in Rome. An act and retribution: Rabbi Hanina was found to have taken the Lord's name in vain. When warned about being punished by the Romans who had forbidden the study of Torah, he too answered "Mercy will come from the Heavens". His own end was without mercy, burnt alive wrapped in the scroll of the Torah. Bruria's mother died because she did not protest her husband's taking the name of the Lord in vain. Bruria's brother died, for "there were those who said he was a traitor". And Bruria's sister was condemned to prostitution because her manner of walking was sexually arousing.

From father-mother-brother-sister the story goes on to deal with "husband" and "sons": the death of Bruria and Rabbi Meir's sons. As in the Midrash source,[40] the story is given detailed emphasis as a realistic incident about Bruria who prepares her husband for news of his sons' deaths, climaxing in a justification of the disaster as "the pledge must be returned to its master" (a sort of equivalent to the fatalistic phrase "Mercy will come from the Heavens"). The reasoning for the death of the sons is only found in the Midrash. In *Midrash Mishle* Rabbi Hama bar Hanina asks: "Why were Rabbi Meir's sons punished and they died suddenly?" And he answers: "Because they were used to abandoning the *Beth Midrash* and eating and drinking." And Rabbi Yochanan adds: "And even performed idle acts." The play does not feature the Midrash debate that "explains" the deaths and lays responsibility upon Bruria as a mother who spoiled her children. The emphasis in this theatrical adaptation is "feminist", as explained by Miller: "Our version diverges fundamentally from the traditional interpretation of the tale. The *mise en scène* 'accuses' Bruria of being tempted to restore the boys to life; this interpretation is based upon a text which recounts that the rabbis were able to resurrect the dead."[41] This scene of bereavement was written in the context of

---

[40] *Midrash Mishle* 31: 10–13.
[41] Miller, note 25, 18.

a "masculine" war which had caused the loss of many lives and aroused much objection and controversy, as the playwright noted:

> The play was put together during the War in Lebanon (1982) and the war provided many new and frightening ramifications for the ancient texts from the Talmud upon which the play is based. The question of personal responsibility and its limits which is raised in the play – scene after scene – becomes a burning issue in war and its aftermath, echoing with renewed relevance in the ancient tales. [42]

The play returns to the wedding scene. There is a familiar repetition of the movements in the scene, in the hair combing and the clear water, which prepares us for the next scene, which is that of Bruria's sister; a moment of deceptive calm, after the horrifying scene which had preceded it, and before Bruria meets her end.

However, before this the play intervenes with a comic element. Bruria asks her husband to save her sister from being condemned to the brothel. Rabbi Meir disguises himself as a cavalryman and arrives at his sister-in-law's without her recognising him; and, because she withstands the test of her purity, she is saved. A comic scene is interwoven here for two men – Rabbi Meir and the brothel guard whom he bribes. According to Gabriella Lev, the text in Aramaic sounds "like an echoing Hebrew, and is also funny in the original due to the situation of a rabbi visiting a brothel." The comedy is helped by an abrupt and fast-paced dialogue. "The mixture of comedy in a tragic story went down well,"[43] noted the director with satisfaction. It is of course possible that the original text[44] tended towards the comic, but it is difficult to avoid the assumption of an (albeit unconscious) attempt to depict the ridiculed male in the instant before he is revealed in all his moral ugliness.

Toward the end of the second part of the play, the first narrator introduces the Rashi version:

> Rashi writes: Once Bruria made fun of the rabbinic dictum "women are frivolous". He [her husband, Rabbi Meir] said: "On your life! You will end up admitting they are right." He commanded one of his students to tempt her into [sexual] transgression. The student importuned her for many days, until in the end she agreed. When the matter became known to her, she strangled herself, and Rabbi Meir fled because of shame.[45]

---

[42] Even the performance of *A Thousand Esthers and Hester* in 1988 against the background of the *intifada* was a criticism of "a policy of force which has overrun Israel particularly in recent times." Aliza Elion-Israeli and Gabriella Lev, "There is an Experimental Theatre in Jerusalem", *Bamah*, 113/114, 1988, 126.

[43] Miller, note 25, 13.

[44] Babylonian Talmud, *Avoda Zara* 18a.

[45] Rashi in the Babylonian Talmud *Avoda Zara* 18b, translated following Boyarin, note 30, 184.

The *Epilogue*, according to Gabriella Lev, is "Bruria's suicide scene. But also our own reaction as story tellers to the pain that it caused us." It comprises pieces from the play and the sources, mainly of its female protagonist. The epilogue, to use Julia Kristava's binary concept, tends towards turning the story from being part of a "symbolic" order into a "semiotic" text which suffers neither from social pressures nor the masculine rules of order.[46]

> (*During this speech Bruria has enacted in stylized movement the betrayal and suicide. The dialogue in the scene that follows is not fixed, nor is it made definite whether the actresses are playing the roles of the storytellers or of Bruria and her sister, or other personage in the play, or themselves, or all or any of these. In the final line of the play they will be designated as storytellers. The scene is open to improvisation. What is said varies from one performance to another. The result is a fragmented retelling of the dramatized story, not necessarily in the order in which the scenes were played. The fragments of dialogue place what was said earlier in fresh contexts. Often sharply ironical. Rashi's comment is always replayed and in challenging fashion*).
>
> [...]
>
> **Gabi**: (*A dance starting from the rhythm of the text*) Rashi writes. Rashi writes that once Bruria made light.
>
> **Ruth**: Made light ... made light.
>
> **Gabi**: Of the saying of the wise that women are fickle minded. And Rabbi Meir said to Bruria take heed. The end of your life will bear witness to their words. And he ordered one of his students to seduce Bruria.
>
> **Ruth**: Bruria, what is it to be the wife of a man?
>
> **Gabi**: And he cajoled her ...
>
> **Ruth**: Bruria, you and Rabbi Meir are like two uprooted mountains standing one against another. Will you crush one another until the end? Or will a quickening of compassion within you let live?
>
> **Gabi**: And he cajoled her. It is a shame for me. And he cajoled her day after day until she gave herself. And when she found out (*goes to the water and washes herself*) and when she found out (*plays with her feet in the water on the floor*) and they brought sponges of wool soaked in water and laid these to his heart to slow the hasting away of his soul.
>
> **Ruth**: Father, must I see you thus?
>
> **Gabi**: If I were made to burn here alone it would be a hard thing for me.
>
> **Ruth**: What do you see?
>
> **Gabi**: I see the world like a clear, clean water. The light and destruction (*begins spilling the water from the bowl*)

---

[46] Julia Kristava, "Interview avec Xavière Gauthier", *Tel Quel*, 58, 1974, 98–102.

Ruth: (*again playing the storyteller, singing*) Water flows, fire flames, and the deed remains locked in the page.
Gabi: (*again playing the storyteller*) This is the story.
(*the stage darkens*)
Blackout
End

The actress accompanies the piece with foot drumming, emphasizing Bruria's rebellious nature. None of this conduces to carthasis. Quite the opposite: it disturbs the impressions of the spectator, who is deluged by statements emphasizing the conflict between man and woman, such as: "Will you crush one another until the end." And it ends in a sort of ritual of spilling water, contrasting with the moulding at the beginning, and a song: "Water flows, fire flames, and the deed remains locked in the page." "This is the story," says the Narrator in her closing line. But this is not the end for the Theatre Company of Jerusalem, for following it and alongside it came the stories of Esther, Sarah and others.

Rachel Adler understands the story of Bruria as an unusual "test case" in which the rabbis are asked the hypothetical question: "What would have happened if a woman like us had existed?" And their brutal answer is found at the end of Bruria's story, which tells two tales – one from the Talmud[47] which she terms a tale of "a virgin in a brothel" about Bruria's sister who preserved her purity even within a Roman brothel; and the other tale which can be found in Rashi about Bruria who, despite her greatness, was only a woman and thus frivolous, and her husband, in order to prove this to her, tricked her with the aid of one of his students. Adler perceives the two "parallel" stories as a "political dream" in which "[…] male superiority and patriarchic power are reinforced by reducing women to their sexual function."[48] According to Boyarin, this story examines the possibility of a woman learning and teaching the law of *halacha* as a distant but nonetheless threatening possibility for the hegemony of male *halachic* culture.[49] The study of Torah was (and still is) a male activity intended to form an almost erotic link with the Torah as if with a woman. The "Torah" and the "wife" are thus perceived within this male culture as separate areas (*ibid.* 196).

The play examines these social conventions in their historical and a-historical connections and leads them from the "taken for granted" situation in the prologue, through the feminist deconstruction in the second and main part, while questioning the stern and unyielding

---

[47] Babylonian Talmud, note 44.
[48] Rachel Adler, "The Virgin in the Brothel and Other Anomalies: Character and Context in the Legend of Beruriah", *Tikkun*, Vol. 3, No. 6, 1988, 104.
[49] Boyarin, note 31, 169.

approach of male religious law, to the epilogue in which the women's voice "semiotically" shatters the "story's" components; and expresses the broken hearts caused by our teachers to Rachel Adler and the creators of *Bruria*. From this aspect the play is a harsh and interesting expression of criticism of Jewish tradition by women's theatre in Israel. This is a theatre which answers Cixous's desire for "a political gesture, with a view to changing."[50]

A sense of tension, emanating from the contradiction that has no solution, accompanies a study of *Bruria*, many clear expressions of which can be found in the text, such as the emphasis on duality in all the components of both form and content, which express the sharp divide between man and woman. The play occasionally evokes among some critics and members of the audience the illusion that it is attempting to solve the problem from a feminist perspective, within the framework of the existing *halacha*; but this is only an intermediate strategy enabling the playmakers to progress in a radical direction. For if *Bruria* is a test case from the male point of view, most assuredly it can also serve as a case study from the female point of view, questioning the spirit and authority of the harsh male *halacha*, as demonstrated three times by the fate of the figures in the story; and from whom no member of the audience can escape. The play aims at revealing *another halacha and a different Judaism*. Not only a Judaism in which there is a place for woman, but a Judaism in which the female spirit guides the way of life.

---

[50] Cixous, note 11, 547.

1. A mask of Rabbi Avraham Shapira, a well-known religious politician, used in the dance prologue to *Tartuffe*, adapted by Yehoshua Sobol and directed by Gedalia Besser at the Haifa Municipal Theatre, 1985. Photo: Morel Drefler

2. *Status Quo Vadis* by Yehoshua Sobol, directed by Edna Shavit at the Haifa Municipal Theatre, 1973. From right to left: Gedalia Besser, Gita Munte, Yossef Bashi, Ilan Dar, Ilan Toren and Ruth Segal. Photo: Yaakov Agor

3. Shmuel Hasfari's *Kiddush*, directed by Hasfari, at the Cameri Theatre, 1985. From right to left: Dov Navon, Yossi Graber, Edna Fliedel. Photo: Haramati

4. Yossef Carmon as the Butcher forced to convert to ultra-Orthodoxy, with Yossi Kantz as Hund, in Igal Even-Or's *Fleischer* directed by Amit Gazit at the Cameri Theatre, 1993. Photo: Haramati

5. *Ish Hassid Haya* by Dan Almagor, directed by Yossi Yzraely, Bimot Theatre, 1968. From right to left: Danny Litany, Batia Barak, Deborah Dotan, Lolik Levy, Shlomo Nizan and Hanna Roth. Photo: Yaakov Agor

אמיר

עריכה ועבוד – דן אלמגור

6. *Bruria* by Aliza Elion-Israeli, directed by Joyce Miller, Theatre Company of Jerusalem, 1982. Gabriella Lev and Ruth Wieder. Photo: Aliza Elion-Israeli

7. *A Night at the Mall* by Orli Castel-Bloom, directed by Oded Kotler, Haifa Municipal Theatre, 1994. A religious married couple of settlers are trapped in the mall, the "palace" of secular and hedonistic Israeli culture. Shragit Bikovsky and Yoav Heit. Photo: Morel Drefler

8a. *Mirkam*, directed by Zippora Luria, Samaria community centre, 1994: The opening scene. Photo: Zippora Luria

8b. *Mirkam*, directed by Zippora Luria, Samaria community centre, 1994: The final monologue by Deborah Recanati. Photo: Zippora Luria

8c. *Mirkam*, directed by Zippora Luria, Samaria community centre, 1994: An audience of religious women only. Photo: Zippora Luria

9. Religious stand-up comedy: Noya Shuster and Nurit Hadar in *Bidur K'Halacha*, directed by Hanan Goldblat, 1994. Photo: Eli Mendel

10. *Nashim b'Yarok* ("Women in Green"). Photo: Nadia Matar

11. *Boochie* by Yossef Bar-Yossef, directed by Gedalia Besser, Haifa Municipal Theatre, 1984. Yossi Polak (left) as Boochie and Michael Kfir as his father. Photo: Morel Drefler

12. Uri Zohar and Hanna Laslow in the film *Save the Lifeguard*, screenplay and direction by Uri Zohar, 1977. This was Zohar's last film, before his conversion to ultra-Orthodoxy. Photo: David Gurfinkel

13. Rabbi Uri Zohar proselytizing. Photo: Viki Cohen

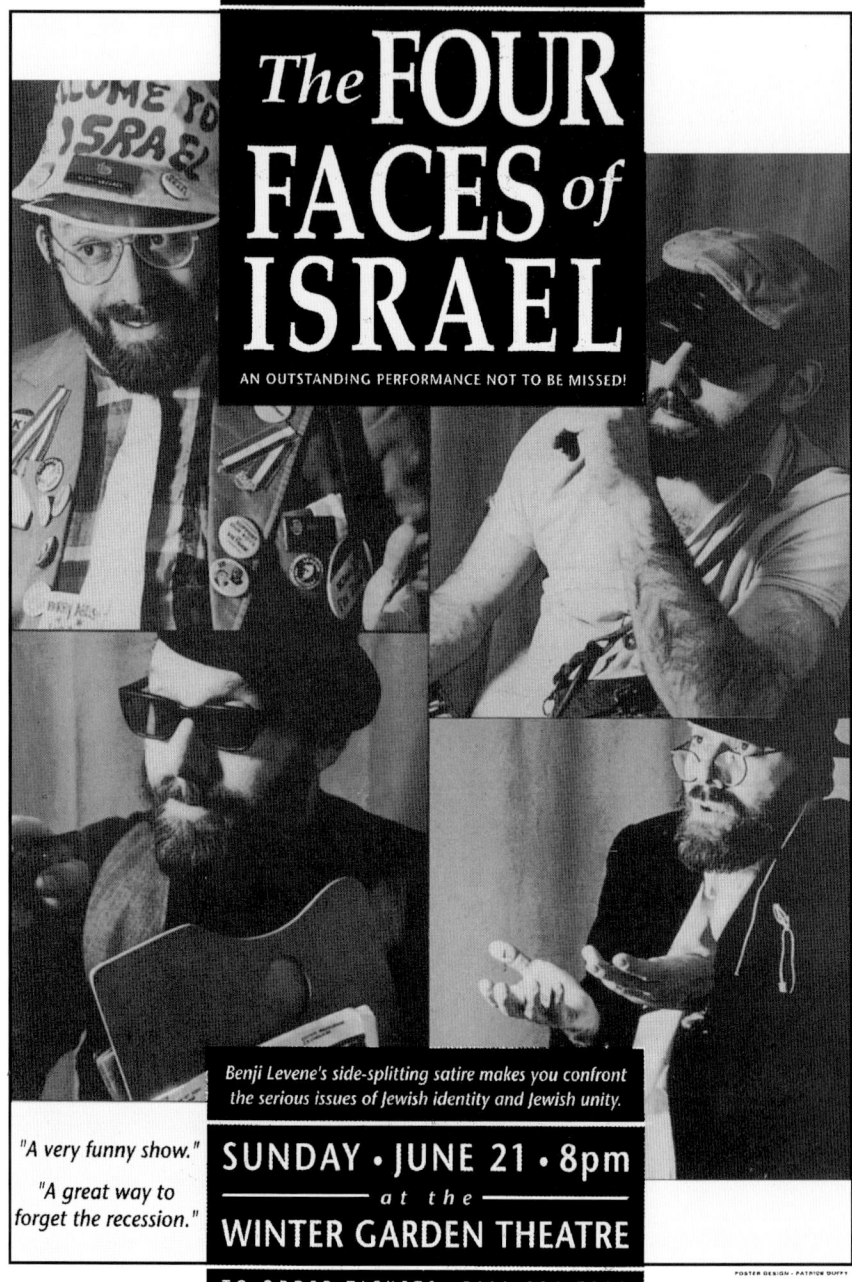

THE GESHER FOUNDATION PRESENTS

The FOUR FACES of ISRAEL

AN OUTSTANDING PERFORMANCE NOT TO BE MISSED!

Benji Levene's side-splitting satire makes you confront the serious issues of Jewish identity and Jewish unity.

"A very funny show."

"A great way to forget the recession."

SUNDAY • JUNE 21 • 8pm
at the
WINTER GARDEN THEATRE

TO ORDER TICKETS • CALL 256-7211

POSTER DESIGN - PATRICK DUFFY

14. Rabbi Benji Levene has performed *The Four Faces of Israel* since 1978. Photo: Patrick Duffy

17. The "anthropological" plays of Amnon Levy, staged to great acclaim, in the 1990s reveal the interest shown by the secular in the religious "Other". *Sheindele* by Levy and Ramy Danon (directed by Danon at the Cameri Theatre, 1993) is about religious women in a male-dominated society. From right to left: Yossi Kantz, Esther Greenberg-Shabak, Orna Porat. Photo: Haramati

תיקון חצות

מאת אמנון לוי ורמי דנון

הקאמרי
של תל-אביב

18. *Midnight Prayer* by Amnon Levy and Ramy Danon (directed by Danon at the Cameri Theatre, 1996) is a play about the mutiny by religious Jews of oriental origin against domination by *Ashkenazi* ultra-Orthodox. In the promotional poster for the play the actor Yoram Chatav is made up to look like a well-known oriental religious politician. Photo: Micha Kirshner

19. Moshe Becker as Hirshel in an adaptation of S. Y. Agnon's *A Simple Tale*, Habima Theatre, 1979. One of Yossi Yzraeli's attempts to deal with his Jewishness through theatre. Photo: Yaakov Agor

20. *Soul of a Jew* by Yehoshua Sobol, directed by Gedalia Besser, Haifa Municipal Theatre, 1982. Doron Tavori as the anti-Semitic Jewish philosopher Otto Weininger. Photo: Yaakov Agor

21. *Teshuva* by Nuriel Tobias, directed by Ilan Toren, Haifa Municipal Theatre, 1997. A new convert to ultra-Orthodoxy, Shaul Mizrachi, confronts secular temptation in the form of a prostitute, Maya Maoz. Photo: Eyal Landsman

4

RELIGIOUS WOMEN'S THEATRE IN ISRAEL

Recent years have seen a growth in the number of theatrical activities by religious-Zionist women in community theatre, stand-up comedy and street theatre. These women present the anxieties of a particular Israeli social group to both "external" secular spectators and the "internal" religious audience. Their theatrical activities raise several questions: (a) regarding their very existence despite the monolithic nature of Israeli theatre, which does not encourage the presence of "other" theatrical expressions; (b) the impossible combination of a religious-Jewish theatre, which is forbidden, thereby creating a sort of cultural oxymoron; and (c) in particular, the theatrical activity of religious Jewish women is a phenomenon which, for social religious reasons, would have been unthinkable only a decade ago. This chapter attempts to explain and answer the question: Why and how was this Pegasus created?

A presentation of the difficulties facing any theatrical event performed by religious women will help us to understand their activities. A religious-Zionist women's theatre cannot constitute a component within the majority culture in Israel, due to the specific nature of the established theatrical system. The Hebrew theatre, since its inception in the 1920s, has been aimed at a specific group, the very same group which is also involved in directing its path. Most of the theatre practitioners and their audience are secular, of western origin, and of above average education. The Israeli theatre "players" – theatre managers, playwrights and directors, are in the main masculine, and belong to the above-mentioned social group. Consequently, the major part of the repertoire (particularly original works) tends to constitute works aimed at answering the problems that occupy this group.

The "us" of Israeli theatre, like the "us" of Israeli "public thought", as characterised by Yona Hadari-Ramage is: "still that of the *Ashkenazi* [western origin] *chalutz* [pioneer], male, white, blond, pure, redeemer of land and nation."[1] This repertoire has little room for "Other" *dramatis personae*, such as women, Arabs, oriental Jews and the religious. These "Others" often appear in the theatre as the spark in a conflict or in their link to the male characters. Consequently, there is an importance above

---

[1] Yona Hadari-Ramage, *Thinking It Over: Conflicts in Israeli Public Thought*, Ramat Efal, Yad Tabenkin and Yediot Aharonot, 1994, 20. (Hebrew)

and beyond that of the theatrical activities themselves, for Israeli audiences perceive the theatre as a preferred place for discussion and "laundering" of problems that concern Israeli society. Furthermore, these theatrical texts are widely echoed by the public by means of "secondary texts", such as the printed and electronic media, and sometimes they reach such political stages as the *knesset* [Israeli parliament].[2]

Theatre in Israel is more highly subsidized than any other cultural area. This subsidy principally reaches mainstream theatre, with fringe theatre receiving a minimal share.[3] In a small country, whose potential audiences are in any case limited, this effectively blocks the development of fringe theatre and restricts the possibilities of other "voices" being heard. It is therefore easy to understand why women's theatre hardly exists (apart from one group), why theatre representing oriental Jewry no longer exists (one attempt was made but did not persevere – "The Kedem Stage"), why Arab-Israeli theatre until the 1990s was a copy of the Hebrew-Israeli theatre and other than a number of experiments (which came up against various establishment objections), failed to provide an "authentic" expression of the Israeli-Palestinian "voice". More recently too, it only offered a hesitant expression, by means of indirect strategies.[4] The "us" of Israeli theatre is thus an extremely powerful cultural mechanism, reproducing itself, and thereby reinforcing the hegemonic practices of the group that finances it, which it in fact seeks to "reflect" and to which it is addressed. In this connection a religious women's theatre will find difficulty in functioning and the only means open to it are the possibility of operating on the fringe, within a local-community or private framework.

An additional difficulty, making religious theatre almost impossible, is that of the Jewish religious law. In the Talmud [the largest body of Jewish law from the 3rd to 6th centuries C.E.] in *Avoda Zara* 18b there is an injunction against making theatre, which is perceived by the rabbis and religious leaders as a place in which strange gods are worshiped, the seat of fools, a place of light-mindedness and licentiousness. It can be assumed that among many of the religious and traditionally observant the argument of ungodliness no longer holds (other than, perhaps, among the ultra-Orthodox who may perceive theatre as a place in which ceremonies of the Israeli-Zionist "civil religion" take place). Despite this

---

[2] See: Dan Urian, "The Polemic Raised by 'Soul of a Jew'", *Bamah*, 100, 1985, 78–87. (Hebrew)

[3] *Summary of Activities of Public Institutions for Culture and Art in Israel in 1994*, 7, The Public Council for Culture and Art, May 1995, 46, 48–51. (Hebrew)

[4] Dan Urian, ed., "Perspectives on Palestinian Drama and Theatre: A Symposium", *Theatre in Israel*, Linda Ben-Zvi, (ed.), The University of Michigan Press, 1966, 323–45.

however, for many among the observant community the theatre is nonetheless still a place of foolishness and obscenity.

Religious women, whose entire way of life is modest and built around the home, have no place in the theatre due to its public nature which cannot safeguard their modesty. The possibility of religious women themselves actually performing and presenting their problems on stage is even more remote, due to the woman's position in Judaism, poignantly characterized by Cynthia Ozick as of lesser value, sub-human: "We see that woman are perceived as lesser and are thereby dehumanized."[5] The explanation for the amazing existence of religious women's theatre, therefore, is linked to the political changes that began in 1992 among the religious-Zionist community.

The ongoing vociferous public discussion in Israel on the subject of the peace agreement with the Palestinians and the extent of the Jewishness of the State of Israel, has been accompanied by a weakening of the overall influence of the religious-Zionist "settlers" from the occupied territories – a group perceived as the elite of religious-Zionist Judaism. Concomitantly a change has occurred in the group's image; a positively depicted image until the government's change to a policy of conciliation. The settlers are described by Baruch Kimmerling as being perceived by both themselves and their admirers, as the heirs to the pioneers – that exemplary image of the *chalutzim*, the first Hebrew settlers: "the place of the pioneering image has been inherited – having linearly skipped history – by the armed religious settler and his hugely pregnant wife surrounded by her large brood of children."[6] The combination of Palestinian uprising, change of government and the interim agreements with the Palestinians led to a dent in this image. A great many Israelis began to see the settlers as a security (and financial) burden and outspoken expressions of such views could be heard from the late Prime Minister, Yitzhak Rabin. The peace process created "the severest pressure upon the spiritual position of this tall, straight cypress, that has no interest or talent for complications," states Rabbi Menachem Fruman, with a hint of self-irony.[7]

The settlers' activities in the occupied areas had been supported by the right-wing government since 1977, but were halted with the return of the left-wing to power in 1992 and by the Oslo accords that threatened the very existence of these settlements, even after the return to power of the right-wing in 1996. Objections to the Oslo accords led the

---

[5] Cynthia Ozick, "Notes Toward Finding the Right Question", *Forum*, 35, 1979, 58.

[6] Baruch Kimmerling, "It Can Also Happen To Us", *Ha'Aretz*, 21 January 1994. (Hebrew)

[7] Rabbi Fruman, one of the settlement rabbis, wrote about the self-perception of the settler: "The religious-nationalist youth is a religious edition of the Zionist vision of the proud and confident *tsabar* [native born Israeli]." Menachem Fruman, "A Cypress Tree with a Skullcap", *Ha'Aretz*, 21 November 1994. (in Hebrew)

different religious-Zionist bodies to organise various public protests and demonstrations, including theatrical ones. The appearance of women as "actresses"/actresses in such events was an innovation which the men (the rabbis) permitted or even encouraged to a degree, due to the political circumstances.

(Secular) theatre productions preceded these changes, and predicted their occurrence. These plays stemmed from the fact that the majority of Israeli playwrights belong to a group which objects to the settlements and to the messianic culture and ideology which nourish them.[8] Four of these plays are set in a future (Utopia or Dystopia, depending on the point of view), in which the settlers will be forced to evacuate the occupied territories. *Tashmad* [in Hebrew an acronym that also means "destruction"] by Shmuel Hasfari, staged at the 1982 Akko Festival (and revived in 1992), already revealed the dangerous aspects of the settlements from the viewpoint of the Israeli left. The play depicts a situation in which the Israeli government yields to an American ultimatum and decides upon a forced evacuation of the settlers. In a bomb-shelter on the stage an ultra-Orthodox male, a religious female settler, a religious maniac and an extremist right-wing secular male gather together and threaten to blow themselves up if the government does not rescind its decision. An insane messianic/group-dynamics develops among them, during which they also burn the Talmud. Finally, the bomb-shelter blows up together with them. A somewhat similar situation is presented in *Pangs of the Messiah* by Motti Lerner, staged at the Cameri theatre in 1987. The depicted events take place in Samaria, after a United States delegation has succeeded in coercing Israel to withdraw from the occupied territories. A family schism arises between the moderates who perceive the settlements as an error, to the extent of accusing themselves of "forcing the end", and the extremists who promise "there will be no retreat in this war. Afterwards there will remain no mosques and no Arabs."[9] This play too ends in tragedy; when one of the family commits suicide. A while later, following the Oslo accords, a play written by David Steinberg was staged by a High School group at the Akko Festival in 1994 (and also broadcast by television's Educational Channel). This already incorporated the impending conflict in its title: *The Clouds of Samaria*. It is a tale of two families in Samaria: religious Jewish settlers and Palestinians, and the conflicts that result from the peace agreements. The characters of the settlers are realistic, less extremist than in the plays by Hasfari and Lerner, and ready for compromise. One of them, a factory

---

[8] Aviezer Ravitzky, *Messianism, Zionism and Jewish Religious Radicalism*, Tel Aviv, Am Oved, 1993, 111–200. (Hebrew)

[9] Motti Lerner, *Pangs of the Messiah*, Tel Aviv, Or-Am, 1988, 104. (Hebrew)

owning religious-Zionist Jew, sells his factory to a Palestinian. Another settler, whose son had been killed in a Palestinian terrorist attack, is prepared to work in the factory despite the change of ownership. However, such cooperation proves to be almost impossible, mainly due to the burden of the past, and the play ends in the murder of a Palestinian activist while he is being handed over to the Israeli army. In the play *A Night at the Mall* by Orli Castel-Bloom staged by the Haifa Municipal Theatre in 1994, the settlers are turned into post-modernist caricatures. The protagonists, Conny and Avigoshen, are a religious married couple who bring together two traumas – past expulsion and the possibility of future expulsion. They are currently settlers in Alon Moreh [one of the first settlements in the occupied territories] and were formerly inhabitants of Yamit [a town in an area captured by Israel and later returned to Egypt and demolished]. They have been trapped in a somnambulistic night at the mall, the "palace" of secular and hedonistic Israeli culture. Castel-Bloom uses the figure of Conny to present everything that she perceives as extremist and ridiculous about the settlers' ideology; particularly their "construction ethos" which sanctifies the physical expansion of Jewish settlement throughout Israel. Conny wants to go back to Yamit, to find the last hammer used to build the town and to copulate with it; it constitutes the symbol of pioneering for her. This derision of the messianic ethos by Castel-Bloom becomes apparent in her devaluation of the verbal pathos of a pioneering-Zionist-religious-messianic vocabulary to the language of the streets, crushing it beneath the act of "fucking":

> **Conny**: [...] Mainly I want to realise my Utopian ideology.
> **Ziva**: If you fuck a hammer.
> **Conny**: It doesn't bother me. If I fuck it, and I'm full of beans while I'm doing it, I'll improve its self-image, and raise its confidence from nothing, where it is right now, and has been since it stopped banging. It'll come inside me, and I'll get pregnant and have little hammers, descendants of the last hammer of Yamit, and I'll be able to say to them: kids, daddy was the last hammer ever to build in Yamit.

Her husband, as husbands tend to be, is not enthusiastic about her plan, but he does share with his wife the same beliefs and opinions; he suggests that she bring the hammer from Yamit to their settlement in the occupied territories:

> **Avigoshen**: I'm sure that if you tell it that you want it to come to Alon Moreh, then it will come in the end. After all, that's also over the Green Line [the Israeli border prior to the 1967 war]. It can remind it of the houses that it once built. Maybe it will also find some others like itself, other hammers. And it will make friends with them.

> **Conny**: I don't think so. It's terribly reserved. And if they also give back
> Alon Moreh I don't think its heart could take another evacuation.

The negative image of the settler as perceived by the Israeli left-wing and its theatre, did not bother the Judean and Samarian settlers when the right-wing government was supporting and even encouraging them. "The settlement ethos" left no room for dealing with "idle matters" like Arts and the Media. However, the change of government led to second thoughts among them in regard to "the Media", including the theatre. Shai Bazak, council spokesman for Judea and Samaria, considers that "we have erred until recently in our approach to the media. In the past we have mainly only had to build. Today we are in the opposition and need to use democratic tools to influence government policy."[10]

This theatrical activity is an expression of political frustration and disappointment in general, and not only of the left; for the peace talks were originally initiated by a right-wing government. The strategy the settlers chose was termed by Israel Harel (editor of the settlers' journal *Nekuda*) "a non-angry protest".[11] This protest was also clear, direct political theatre, intended to enhance the already-existing fears among Jewish Israelis regarding the Palestinians. Richard Schechner, who called such events "direct theatre", explained that including them under the title "theatre" was not merely metaphorical. Their audiences are: "the participants themselves, journalists, especially television reporters, the mass spectatorship TV enjoys, and high-level decision makers"[12] who are brought face to face with the political dilemmas and standpoints by means of short theatrical texts inserted into the news broadcasts.

Two "representations" (as their initiators called them) were presented in the second half of 1993 at the initiative of the Judea–Samaria Council. One was aimed against what was at the time still only an idea – the establishment of the Palestinian police; while the other attempted to warn against the "return" of a million Palestinians to the borders of Israel. Both events were well planned and co-opted such means as Palestinian police uniforms, police vehicles and even a boat, in order to manifest the dangers and the settlers' objections to the government's policy, in front of the television cameras.[13] It would appear that the political reality, and in particular the progress being made in the peace process, had forced the organizers of these two "representations" to adopt other – and

---

[10] From an interview with me (D.U.). After the political reversal in 1996, Bazak became spokesman for the right-wing government.

[11] Hanna Kim, "Gushinkianim", *Hadashot*, 13 August 1993. (Hebrew)

[12] Richard Schechner, "The Street is the Stage", in: *The Future of Ritual: Writings on Culture and Performance*, London and New York, Routledge, 1993, 86–88.

[13] Dan Urian, "Theatre and the *Intifada*", *Contemporary Theatre Review*, Vol. 3, Part 2, 1995, 215–6.

as they saw it more powerful – means in their struggle: mass demonstrations, hunger strikes, blocking of road junctions.

Theatrical activity, however, did not stop there. The stage – with its male actors – was cleared and their place was taken by women. Were women "permitted" or given the authority to carry out theatrical activities because this might be a "suitable" form of expression for them? Or was it perhaps that women were perceived in religious writings as "frivolous" and therefore their contravention of religious law would be slighter? In particular there were pragmatic reasons: they might in fact further the cause in the struggle against the outside and improve the settlers' image among the secular public. They were enlisted to battle the "hostile media" and used its constant hunger for the unusual to present the views of their own group. These theatrical activities were also aimed at strengthening the bonds of a community also facing internal difficulty with the religious-Zionist public (living within the Green Line), some of whom had recurring doubts regarding the settlement ideology.

The inherent difficulties of presenting theatre in a religious-Jewish framework, particularly women's theatre, found a solution (or permit) in the concept that theatre is permissible and even desirable as a tool adopted for the needs of the community "internally" or as a propaganda device for "external" audiences. Rivka Manowicz refers to this, after delineating a firm boundary between theatre as "a place of licentiousness" and theatre as religious Jewish culture. She suggests the creation of an instrumental religious theatre:

> A *tool* [emphasized in the original] for God's work and education to his glory. This is theatre in "chains" but I am not ashamed of declaring this theatre to be "didactic" theatre, "committed". I do not see such adjectives, terms of abuse in the secular world, as disgraceful, but committed to the Creator of the Universe.[14]

The "didactic" nature of this women's theatre is already apparent from the titles of the groups and their plays. "A title is always a promise" states Jacques Derrida.[15] These titles are in themselves "headings": *Nashim b'Yarok* ["Women in Green"], *Mirkam* ["Tissue"], and *Bidur k'Halacha* ["Great Entertainment" or in its double meaning in Hebrew "Entertainment as Religious Law"] are loaded titles. Two of them are based upon a sort of ironic oxymoron: the name "Women in Green" refers to the *Nashim b'Shachor* ["Women in Black"] – a women's

---

[14] Rivka Manowicz, "The Call for a 'Committed' Jewish Theatre", *Dimui*, 5–6, 1993, 22. (Hebrew)

[15] Jacques Derrida, *Memoires: for Paul de Man*, trans. Cecile Lindsay, Jonathan Culler and Eduardo Cadava, New York, Columbia University Press, 1986, 115.

movement whose ideology seeks territorial compromise, in contrast to that of the "Women in Green"; "Great Entertainment" is almost a contradiction in terms, converting the sublime to the lowly in religious daily life, thereby stimulating interest, but also promising to remain within the permitted boundaries; while *Mirkam* is aimed at the world of women (from "embroidery" *rikma*) as well as the fragmentary-interwoven nature of the play.

The female initiators of these various performances have no connection with each other, other than their need for male permission. The street theatre of Nadia Matar ("Women in Green") is a personal/ family enterprise that only later gained retroactive recognition by the male leadership, as expressed by their inviting Matar to appear before the Judea–Samaria council, the organizing body for action against the Oslo accords. The community theatre of Zippora Luria at the Samaria community centre is supported by a legal ruling by the Rabbi of Alon Moreh. Noya Shuster and Nurit Hadar's stand-up show requested and received the blessing of several rabbis.[16]

Directed Inwards

In October 1989 (two years after the outbreak of the *intifada*) the Ganei Tal settlement in Gush Katif (near Gaza) celebrated its first decade. The invited guests included the President of the State of Israel, Chaim Herzog, who congratulated the settlement but also warned against acts of violence from the religious-Zionist public. The settlement, part of the religious-Zionist movement, had prepared a play for the occasion, directed by Roni Aviram. One of the first scenes was of an Arab dressed in dark clothing and accompanied by a camel, speaking broken Hebrew (exchanging 'b' for 'p') and describing the Jews as crazy people who "think that something is going to grow in the middle of the desert." He then renounces the rights of the Arabs to these sand dunes and "gives" them to the new pioneers whose problematic settlement in the area is depicted in the following scenes. The play is reminiscent of the kibbutz plays of the 1930s and 1940s. In the scene following the Arab's appearance, the entire settlement appears on three stages, dressed in festive white: women, men, and children in separate groups. The community sings the song of construction and progress as an antithesis of the Arab who represents desolation and backwardness. The rhetorical conventions (which

---

[16] Noya: "It was important to me that the rabbi should know what we are doing [...] one rabbi read all our texts and laughed, and said that although some things were borderline, we hadn't crossed the border." Assapha Peled, "The Debbie and Nolli of the Religious Community", *Yediot Aharonot*, 18 March 1994. (Hebrew)

shape the theatrical, according to Elizabeth Burns)[17] of organisation of space over several large stages, and the white costumes of the settlement population, in contrast to the black robe of the Arab, embodied the community's sense of achievement and security. Many changes have taken place since then, particularly escalation of the *intifada* as a national Palestinian uprising that cannot be suppressed, the Oslo accords, and the withdrawal of the Israeli army from nearby Gaza, leaving a heavy shadow over Ganei Tal and the other settlements in Gush Katif.

Five years later (1994) the play *Mirkam*, directed by Zippora Luria, was staged by the women's community theatre at the Samaria community centre. This was a reaction by religious Zionism in Samaria and Judea to the Oslo accords. This group's perception of the political changes was clearly formulated by one of its leaders, Yoel Bin-Nun:

> Through the efforts of the settlement in Judea and Samaria in the past 27 years [...] there has been an attempt to create an irreversible reality, through sharp polarization [...] now the other side is trying to establish an irreversible historical reality by means of force, with a clear effort to silence its opponent, to break its spirit and to destroy its power.

Bin-Nun is convinced that the most serious schism in Israel society ("the breaking point") is not between western and eastern Jews, or between the religious and the secular, but:

> between the national-religious in their radical-Zionist expression – "the Great Israel" – on the one hand, and the western-secular with their radical liberals and post-Zionism (the radical left), on the other. This conflict is currently a dangerous threat to Israeli society.[18]

Zippora Luria, who lives in the settlement of Ofra, describes the crisis in more personal terms. She feels "like a political person since the Oslo accords [...] things have happened and we are in trouble [...] everything is overshadowed by uncertainty: you don't know where you're going to be in a short time from now."[19] Luria began to take an interest in "happenings" at the end of the 1970s. As a director and art critic she was interested in experimental works in the arts and particularly theatre. She had also directed *Hegel's Variations* by Gabriel Moked (1982) at a theatrical workshop: a text of poetry and philosophy that was "suitable for

---

[17] Elizabeth Burns, *Theatricality: a Study of Convention in the Theatre and in Social Life*, New York, Harper and Row, 1973, 40–121.

[18] Yoel Bin-Nun, "Disintegration of Identity", *Dimui*, 8, Summer 1994, 14. (Hebrew)

[19] From an interview with me (D.U.). Additional quotes from the interview will not be specified hereafter.

experimentation". Since moving to live in the occupied territories, she
has worked as a director in the region. One of her works was "the biography of Brenner" by Danny Horowitz, *The Story of Yehezkel Fierman*
(1988): "It was clear that we wouldn't take a play by Hanoch Levin. The
spiritual mood of the settlers is not one of shattering and alienation; but
we sought instead a tale with empathy for the story of pioneering
Zionism." The play was staged during the *intifada* and served to reinforce the settlers. "We learned to come to terms with the *intifada*," noted
Luria, "but Oslo was a worse blow. The *intifada* had been created by the
Arabs. Oslo was created by the Israeli government."

Mirkam was the enterprise of the "hard core" of religious Zionist
settlers in Samaria – a group of women from Alon Moreh who were
joined by women from other settlements. Together with Luria, they
determined the formula for this women's theatre that performed for
women: "the feminine structure is determined by issues of religious law.
This is not 'feminist' theatre but Jewish-religious-feminine theatre." The
play was born during the early stages of work, when the participants
were asked to prepare an autobiographical monologue as an exercise,
which then became the basis upon which the work was continued:

> We did not undertake to provide a "well-made" play with several acts:
> exposition, complication and resolution. I wanted an experimental
> theatre – unique, interesting and unusual.

The theatrical text comprises mainly monologues. Luria edited
all the material and chose a suitable pattern for the play. This is a community theatre whose participants are all women with large families; so
when one of the actresses is unable to appear for any reason her scene
is simply cut. From the sociological theatrical point of view, *Mirkam*
provides an interesting document. On the one hand the rhetorical (theatrical) conventions belong to the syntax of experimental and alternative
theatre – being anti-realistic, fragmented, with symbolic rather than
mimetic scenery, and the use of masks and symbolic props. On the other
hand the authenticating conventions (representing social reality, according to Elizabeth Burns), resemble the world of the actresses themselves,
who recount their lives and experiences in their own words. Even the
costumes approximate their normal daily wear: the dress and head
covering which for some of the religious audience arouse associations of
purity and fulfilment.

The opening scene principally indicates the tension between
structure and contents. The "pre-performance" is a manifesto – one of the
participants appears on stage, weaving on a loom; she turns to the audience
and says: "You want to know who I am? I am my brother/my father/my
mother/my grandfather/my grandmother/in my settlement/they are all

me." This is a declaration of intentions in stark contrast with the "I" of secular, individualist theatre, at least as it is depicted among the religious. The opening scene continues with a women's choir, dressed in black, their faces masked, who turn to the audience and recite in unison (climaxing in a shout):"approaching/disappointed/returning/excited/praying/*settling*." This is a didactic performance that despite being directed mainly inwards, is also meant for a secular audience as well as for the religious-Zionist one within the Green Line, and is intended to refute the stereotype of the settler:

> This play, the actresses and director Zippora Luria will tell you, is intended to dispose of the stigma that has stuck to the inhabitants of Judea and Samaria, beginning with the unusual name ["settlers", D.U.] for a group of people whose settlement days have been long forgotten and who today are veteran residents of their various townships; and ending with this uniform perception with which they have been labeled.[20]

Most of the scenes are "storytelling theatre", with the exception of one scene which appears to have been taken from a kibbutz play, and which contains a comic conflict between the absorption committee of one of the settlements and a family of "city folk" who have applied for membership. The resemblance to a kibbutz is not coincidental. Several of the actresses are ex-kibbutz members. The glorious pioneering tradition represented by the kibbutz in the past has now been transferred to these settlements, that exemplify, according to their own perception, pioneering at the end of the 20th century.

The narrators/characters have several elements in common; particularly their attitude to men. Men are "missing" from all the scenes and sketches in the play, but their presence is strongly felt nonetheless, offstage as well as in its contents. "They are in the background, as 'significant figures'," states Luria. It is they who permit the play to be performed and their wives to participate in it. The male dominance is especially felt in one young woman's tale of her return to the religious Jewish fold, following her husband, because she feared losing him. Another common and recurrent element in the play is to be found in expressions of the sense of isolation and alienation from Israeli society that increased following the positive acceptance of the Oslo accords among Israeli society: "We live here in relative isolation, you know, and we have a great need for friendship," says one of the characters. The most important common element to all the scenes is the political one. This is a political play aimed at strengthening and convincing the already convinced, which it achieves

---

[20] Yaffa Goldstein, "*Mirkam* against the 'Settler' Stigma", *Ha'Zofeh*, 9 December 1994. (Hebrew)

by narrative means, mainly using language to extol the settlers' lives. "The people here are people of pathos", says Luria, "and who is to say that this is bad? To be a believer in this century could be considered anachronistic." (*ibid*).

Several of the scenes are overtly political, recounting the physical conflict with the secular and telling of the murder of a child by Arabs. The Arabs themselves do not appear in the play, but represent an anonymous threat.[21] In one monologue the narrator reconstructs a traumatic journey to give birth at the hospital: "Careful. Be careful at this bend. As long as they don't throw stones at us here. I couldn't stand the shame." Such repressed fears are also revealed in the monologue of a woman waiting for her husband to arrive on the bus from Jerusalem. She attempts to determine by telephone whether the bus has been attacked. The monologue is comic in nature, despite the subject matter; it makes the audience laugh, and also possibly releases their fears. A more explicit tale is told by Rami Haba's teacher. Rami is the child who was murdered by Palestinians. A schoolbag lies on a chair. A memorial candle and a choir seeking the child – a choir that does not mention the origin of the murders: "Sons of darkness murdered you, a pure and innocent child," and there remains "only an orphaned chair and a broken heart."

An overt (and painful) conflict is that with the Israeli soldier who must forcefully evict the demonstrators from the roadway:

> Yesterday we went down to Hawara, the Arab village next to Alon Moreh, we went to demonstrate, we blocked the road. We were simply fed up with having stones thrown at us! The soldiers arrived straight away. So did the regional commander. It was terrible. "Hang on, what's going on here? Don't shove! Why are you hitting? Say something. Hey ... you're ... trampling ... him! Give me your details! [...]" I would say to him: "Soldier, we sent you cakes for the Sabbath. Have a flower perhaps. A rose ... it's beautiful, a cold drink? I'm not angry over what's happened. You are carrying out your duty. Nonetheless ... have some chocolate perhaps? It's sweet ... "

The majority of the scenes feed on pathos: a pathos of the pioneering land myth that returns the texts to the original period of settlement, the Zionist play and the framework of the 1930s and 1940s; a pathos supported by the use of rhetorical Hebrew – unique to this group, spiced with religious expressions. The source of this particular rhetoric can be found in the tension between the threatening, uncertain, controversial

---

[21] In the local Judea–Samaria newspaper a critic notes that she found the play lacking in "reference to the Arab who lives alongside us – an issue that demands to be heard (please not at the political level) when the subject is 'Samarian' theatre." Mira Keydar, "The Weaving of *Mirkam* and Women's Organisation", *Nekudah*, May 1995, 43. (Hebrew)

reality, and the ideology of those believers who are proceeding, according to their perception, "leading the camp and lighting its way," on the way to redemption.[22] However, most of the "camp" (the Jewish community in Israel) do not appear to be continuing on the same path, and even digress from it in a totally different direction. The bridge between disappointing reality and appealing reality is created by means of the language and symbols of the struggle, including exemplary figures. Religious-messianic myth and language in the play enable confrontation with harsh issues. One interesting example is the final (and summarizing) monologue by Deborah Recanati. The links between her actual life, which is well known in the Judea–Samaria settlements, and her staged monologue enhance its theatrical effect. She has ten children, is the wife of a rabbi, makes a living from agriculture, and makes frequent public appearances before women who have returned to the religious fold. Her entire life experience has been a sort of conscious continuation of the stream of biblical mothers and *chalutzot*, the female pioneers from the first period of emigration [beginning in 1882]. Her appearance is simple and her pathos direct: "We were born in 1948 – the State and I" are her opening words. Her biography equals a sort of brief history of the ideology of *Gush Emunim* [the group of religious-Zionist settlers in the occupied territories] prior to the 1967 war and following it. This is a dialogue lacking any personal dimension, despite its apparent intent to recount Deborah's life story. The monologue tells of a group of young men and women who saved

> themselves from the compromising image that had stuck to their ancestors for the past three generations – that of "middlemen" sitting on the fence between the ultra-Orthodox and the secular [...] and took their birthright into their own hands. In other words: despite the ultra-Orthodox thesis, focused on the past, and despite the anti-thesis of the secular, focused against the past, they will present the redeeming synthesis turned toward the future (*ibid.*, 170).

For Recanati the collective "I" takes precedence over the individual and "the general needs are her needs" states Zippora Luria. The scene itself is paved with transitions from the mundane to its religious-Zionist-messianic, theological justification. It mixes the vernacular with rhetoric, quotations from religious sources and pioneering-Zionist sources. The monologue creates what Umberto Eco terms "a unique semantic field"[23] – an ideological dialogue, which mixes two religions: Judaism and the

---

[22] Ravitzky, note 8, 170.
[23] Umberto Eco, *Segno*, Milano, Isedi, 1973, 156.

Israeli-Zionist civil religion.[24] This is a dialogue that relates to the contrasting, liberal, secular dialogue, and attains its uniqueness through emphasizing the difference. (Recanati says about her children: "The children are educated to manual labour, bright, gifted children." And, they are contrasted with the secular "Other": "him with the earring in his ear and a beer can in his hand.") Her words also reflect her attitude in a persuasive monologue regarding other groups: the (secular!) female pioneers from the first wave of immigration; the army unit which evicts demonstrators as well as the secular fellow with the earring. She assimilates them all into her own world while lending them legitimacy by her almost missionary-like forgiveness. All this is performed without any hesitation; without using such means as paradox or irony that characterise the secular-liberal discourse. Everything is clear and there is no doubt that the rhetoric may be stripped away to reveal the mythical foundations that lie beneath this dialogue. The monologue finds sparks of holiness in the mundane, in hard labour, in the danger presented by the Arabs, in the demonstrations and political struggle. It is these that provide Recanati, from the cosmic, kabbalistic perspective, with a sense of possessing the right to dream about "redeeming the world through the worship of God", to whom all her actions are directed:

> (*costumed as a pioneer*)
> Near the house where I lived – 18 Rothschild Street in Tel Aviv – they declared the establishment of the State of Israel.
> Grandfather's house
> [...]
> Father always used to tell about life in Kfar Etzion, Kfar Etzion which fell on the eve of the establishment of the State. Afterwards we were a happy group of students who enlivened all the meetings of former members of *Lehi* [one of the Jewish underground organisations, prior to the establishment of the State, which fought mainly against the British]. We made sure to close all the shutters – as befits members of the underground – in 1967! We dreamed about founding a great national movement and talked about Shechem, Hebron and Jerusalem. At the university they called us "messianic". That was the same year that the Six Day War broke out. We liberated Judea, Samaria and the Golan Heights.
> And we returned to father's Gush Etzion.
> [...]
> It's not easy to manage a large household, to hitchhike to work [...] to be the wife of an agriculturist...
> An agriculturist's wife?! A *yeshiva* student, an educator...
> [...]

---

[24] Charles S. Liebman and Eliezer Don-Yehiya, "The Dilemma of Reconciling Traditional Culture and Political Needs: Civil Religion in Israel", in *Religion and Politics in Israel*, Bloomington, Indiana University Press, 1984, 46–48.

Have to prepare flowers for shipment, have to go to the demonstration in Jerusalem, have to participate in the education committee, have to close the car blinds on the way.
Have to be patient.
Have to bend for each and every flower.
[...]
At first there were myrtle trees, anemones. The authorities didn't take us seriously: "Gush Emunim – they're all talk." But we went on working with our spades just like in the old days, in an age of fax machines and microwaves ...
"Effort and more effort and the mountains begin to bear fruit.
(*singing*)
Dear land, on which we built
blessed property, you no longer belong to strangers
I shall give you all my strength ..."
Who's that? That's not my voice. Another voice is speaking from within me, the voices of the pioneering women of the nation.
[...]
I am here, with dreams of arousing the world's redemption through works of God.
I am here in the flurry and flow, left hand striking the right. Right hand returning the blow, all the body shocked and shaken and the heart weeping.
[...]
And we must go on harvesting and restraining ourselves
for the soldier who pushed us at the crossroads – he is my brother.
And the one with the earring and beer can in his hand – he too is my brother ...
Onward, onward, deeper, deeper, to believe and to love.

Mirkam is generally performed before audiences of the already convinced, who agree with the Gush Emunim version of religious-Zionist views; it ends with a direct appeal to the spectators to join in the singing, almost ceremonially. The actresses sing in unison: "Shake off the dust. Dress yourself in splendid clothing, O bride ..." – a song of welcome for the Sabbath, that among the religious audience arouses associations of the purity and holiness bound up with the life of an observant woman. According to the accounts of various female spectators the song also succeeds in stirring such emotions due to its proximity to Deborah Recanati's monologue.

Questionnaires given to and completed by the audience of religious-Zionist women at two of the performances,[25] reveal the affinity between the play's viewpoint and the beliefs and opinions of its audience. Of the 92 questionnaires returned (about half the spectators for

---

[25] The questionnaires were prepared and distributed by my student Yael Ruppman-Keydar; several of her discerning comments assisted my "reading" of the play.

the two performances), 82 define themselves as religious-Zionist. Over 50 expected a (religious) political play. Their attitude to the monologues presented wavered from appreciative (40) to sympathetic (22) to appreciative and sympathetic (21). The play was perceived as strengthening right-wing political views by half the audience (46); and by a third of the audience (surprisingly) as strengthening feminist views (30). This latter finding is particularly interesting, considering that the male world that had granted these women their "permit" to perform, as a "tool" in the system directed by the religious settlers of Judea and Samaria against the Oslo accords, had also "released" a demon – the female "voice" which until then had remained almost unheard among this group.

Directed Inwards and Outwards

The religious-Zionist public is not entirely homogenous. It includes some groups which do not support settlement in the territories, as well as different approaches to issues such as that of women's status. One interesting expression of this can be found in the stand-up comedy of two young observant women, Noya Shuster and Nurit Hadar. Both are graduates of the Bnei Akiva religious youth movement, attended religious schools and served in the army. They are exceptional in that they continued their studies at the Department of Theatre Arts of Tel Aviv University (the "stronghold of artistic freedom"[26]) and their performances involve that "secular yuppie" genre – stand-up comedy.

Stand-up comedy has begun to flourish within the Israeli cultural system, mainly in the 1990s.[27] Shosh Weitz describes this genre in Israel as a theatrical sub-culture:

> Stand-up comedy performances are staged in small, informal halls; they have no fixed written text and are produced through dialogue between the performer and the audience, which functions in an active role and influences the shape of the occurrence. The performers generally deal with local affairs, and nearly all performers make use of a vulgar vernacular, with constant sexual references [...] It can be seen as an opposing factor to legitimate theatre (*ibid.*, 90).

Philip Auslander refers to the important and interesting role played by stand-up in connection to women:

> Our society sees joke telling as an unacceptably aggressive behaviour for women [...] Joke telling is a male preserve because humor is linked

---

[26] Peled, note 16.

[27] In a 1990 survey this genre comprised 21% of all the plays staged in the Israeli theatre. Elihu Katz *et al.*, *Leisure Culture in Israel: Changes in Types of Cultural Activity 1970–1990*, Jerusalem, Guttman Institute for Applied Social Research, Centre for Information and Research of the Public Council for Culture and Art, 1992, part 3, 56. (Hebrew)

with power; women are supposed to be the objects of jokes, not joking subjects [...] The frequent appearance of women on the stand-up comedy stage is a breakthrough with genuine social implications which may highlight a realignment of gender roles within our society [...] For a women to do stand-up comedy at all, given its traditional identification with male dominance, may be a political act in itself.[28]

In the Israeli theatre system stand-up comedy may have an important function. It provides a framework for young actors and writers who have not found their place in the mainstream to express themselves and appear, albeit before a restricted audience but also before audiences who do not otherwise attend the theatre. Stand-up, at least in Israel, enables youngsters, women, Arabs and the religiously observant to give voice; and this takes place against the conservative theatrical background which we have already described.

In connection to religious-Zionist society, the appearance of two young women in the theatre is most assuredly an innovation, which should be studied from two aspects: "directed inwards" and "directed outwards". Regarding the "within", the very fact that observant women perform before mixed religious audiences of men and women is in itself enough to reinforce the process of change taking place among this group in regard to women's status. Despite the necessity for rabbinical approval, such a performance is nonetheless an exceptional political act, as attested to by one of the performers, Noya Shuster:

> There's a problem with theatre and Judaism. Theatre is passions, intrigues, sex, none of which have a place in Judaism. There's a problem of what to do in such theatre. What conflicts to present, and even if there are conflicts, there are no playwrights and writers, for in religious society there is no awareness of theatre for it has no importance. We have come for the first time to try and break through the boundaries.[29]

The solution these two actresses have found for the religious and social obstacles, is an evening of stand-up comedy comprising sketches "without vulgarity. Without plunging necklines." Ironically, they have chosen a genre which in Israeli culture serves the secular fringe. It suits their needs in its distance from "theatre" and its great flexibility. An additional reason for their choice is cultural: the religious public is used to religious assemblies, in which the sermonizing rabbi is also a sort of actor in the encounter between himself and his audience in a theatrical

---

[28] Philip Auslander, "Comedy about the Failure of Comedy: Stand-up Comedy and Postmodernism", in *Critical Theory and Performance*, eds. Janelle G. Reinelt and Joseph R. Roach, Ann Arbor, University of Michigan Press, 1992, 205.
[29] Peled, note 16.

experience, providing a kind of precedent and even authorization. The actresses do indeed wear men's clothing over their dresses and give short and amusing sermons, including one on the source of the name "secular":

> **Noya**: For some reason, we the observant need to be not only a light for the *goyim* [non Jews], but also, moreover, mainly a light for the Jews.
> **Nurit**: They examine us with a magnifying glass.
> **Noya**: For after all the Bible was written just for us, the religious.
> **Nurit**: The secularists weren't there. Where in fact were they?
> **Noya**: We advanced to the foot of Mount Sinai and they remained behind.
> **Nurit**: Why?
> **Noya**: Because of the tranquility.
> **Nurit**: Hey … they chased it.
> **Noya**: Yes, they got stuck in the sands.
> **Nurit**: That's why they're called secular … [in Hebrew a play on the words *cholani* (sandy) and *chiloni* (secular)].

The play Bidur k'Halacha ["Great Entertainment" or in its double meaning as "Entertainment as Religious Law"] (1994) was put together in collaboration with a secular director, Chanan Goldblatt, and it is aimed mainly at a religious audience, although also as an "mission" to a secular one; it too is didactic theatre: "To show the secularists, that they are missing out" (ibid). At the end of the play the secularists are offered: "Perhaps we can just be ordinary people together/if not like a pair of doves, at least like a divorced couple/who know that despite the division there is also something that unites." The actresses attempt to convince the secularist to abandon his stereotyped notion of the religious Jew, despite the fact that to the religious audience, ironically, they themselves present secularism as a particularly stupid antithesis. The degree of aggression often exhibited in the humour directed from "us" (actors and audience) towards the "Other" – is in this case aimed at the secularists, like the above-quoted sermon on the source of the name *chiloni* [secular]. Two of the sketches depict the secular in their eager search to find meaning in their life within cults that promise them eternal life and happiness; or engulfed in superstition and frequenting fortune-tellers, such as the "reader" of rice grains. They take these paths despite the availability of the one true path – the Jewish religion. A special sketch is devoted to the oriental (in this case Moroccan) secular Jew, here represented as frivolous, shallow, unctuous, adulterous, a liar and ignorant. In this sketch an oriental married man attempts to court a young religious girl. He is depicted from his costume to his accent as a negative stereotype. The observant and the secular meet up during festivities and family celebrations, such as a bar-mitzvah. One of the scenes depicts a secular couple at a bar-mitzvah in the synagogue. The woman, who is not familiar with the local customs, is swift to throw candies even before the sermon is over. The thoughts of the secular husband are heard in "voice-over" against the background of the prayer reading, revealing the shallowness, boredom, materialistic nature and ignorance that characterise him:

> Oof, where did I put the car keys? [...] Okay, I'll try and pray a bit. Where is it? I've lost my place [...] I'm dying to go to the bathroom [...] That bar-mitzvah kid's so ugly [...] (he gazes at his shoes in satisfaction) These shoes – a great buy. Cheap, only pinch a bit [...] it's taking ages [...] a bar-mitzvah is the longest thing they ever invented in religion.

Preparation of the play was accompanied by many deliberations regarding the material dealing with the status of observant women. Noya notes: "There was an idea of doing a scene about male chauvinism in Judaism, but I didn't agree."[30] One of the sketches, however, does deviate from the others in criticizing religious matchmaking practices and the entire marriage brokerage "business":

> **Mother:** This is my son, Chaim Moshe. He's eighteen today.
> **Matchmaker:** *Mazal Tov* [congratulations]
> [...]
> **Mother:** Have you found anyone?
> **Matchmaker:** Number 17.
> **Mother:** Hanna Beilah?
> **Matchmaker:** A wonderful girl.
> **Mother:** Talented?
> **Matchmaker:** Very.
> **Mother:** Well-bred?
> **Matchmaker:** Wonderfully.
> **Mother:** Medical health certificates?
> **Matchmaker:** Already dealt with.
> **Mother:** Would you recommend her?
> **Matchmaker:** Highly.
> **Mother:** I'll take her.
> **Matchmaker:** Impossible.
> **Mother:** Why?
> **Matchmaker:** She's already promised.
> **Mother:** Final?
> **Matchmaker:** No.
> **Mother:** Why?

---

[30] From an interview with me (D.U.).

Matchmaker: They haven't paid.
Mother: So, well …
Matchmaker: No problem. First come first served. Tell me, how's your
    Mottel?
Mother: Fine. Thank you.
Matchmaker: Why am I asking? 'Cause there's a special offer. Two for
    the price of one. Whoever takes Hanna Beilah gets Reisel at half-price
    and a key-ring.

Directed Outwards

Nashim b'Yarok ["Women in Green"] is a women's organisation founded
in reaction to the Oslo accords; it contrasts with the other women's
organisation – *Nashim b'Shachor* ["Women in Black"], that during the
Lebanon War and the *intifada* demonstrated against the right-wing and
the national coalition government. The central figure in this organisation
is Nadia Matar, a traditionally observant woman who lives with her
family in Efrat, a settlement in the occupied territories inhabited by both
religious and secular Jews. The female members of this organisation are
not all religious-Zionist, despite which Matar was "adopted" by the
Judea–Samaria council (composed of religious males), apparently due to
their theatrical success.

Matar describes her "credo" with the simplicity that also characterises the theatre she creates:

> I believe in one single axiom: the Jewish nation has a right to exist. Judea,
> Samaria and Gaza should be annexed to Israel and the Arabs given the
> rights of foreign residents. With no right to vote for parliament. They
> want to be Palestinians and live among us, okay. On condition that there
> will be no terrorism.[31]

Matar's success in activating the media has benefited her ability as a
director of street theatre. "Street theatre is one of our greatest achievements. We quickly realised that people in the street are in a hurry, they
don't have time to read texts on placards; that it isn't effective when we
just stand there with our banners and shout out our message. It needs
greater visual impact" (*ibid*). This approach is aimed not just against the
political methods of "Women in Black", but also against the theatrical
rhetorical conventions they employed: women dressed in black and carrying placards of protest, with no "dramatic" activity whatsoever. Matar
understands the needs of the media, and particularly of television, which

---

[31] Dalia Karpel, "She has to Shout Gevalt", *Ha'Aretz*, 27 January 1995. (Hebrew)

require instantly comprehensible material, preferably tending toward the dramatic.[32]

Street theatre by the "Women in Green" is staged with careful choice and planning of organisation of space, costumes, masks, large puppets, placards and megaphones. The performances themselves are organised as short narratives given one after the other in the same location. The texts present such scenes as the hanging of Arafat, a public trial for Itzhak Rabin, a Nobel prize ceremony, a test taken by released Palestinian prisoners following the Oslo accords, and more. The chosen performance locations are generally main streets or squares in Tel Aviv and Jerusalem. The announcer loudly proclaims the event and some of the participants, costumed, carrying placards and accompanied by large puppets and masks of the main actors: Rabin, Peres, Arafat, Hussein...grab the attention of passers-by. The most important addressees of these shows are the journalists, who have arrived by prior invitation, and who do indeed film, record and broadcast them in Israel and around the world. This is "direct theatre" particularly suited to the needs of television – short, simple drama, sharply expressed; and an occasional clash with the police only serves to heighten its news value. One example of this is the sketch "The Dome of the Rock" staged in a main square in Jerusalem, that presented the ban on ten Jews from entering the area at one time, in order to avoid the possibility of their creating a *minyan* [quorum for prayer] and praying there. Some who wish to enter – King Hussein, Arafat and his aids, receive the blessing of Rabin and Peres; while a couple of Christian tourists are not permitted entry. A conflict develops between the tourists and a policeman, at the end of which the show's moderator turns to the audience to rouse them to the injustice taking place. This short (a few minutes) dramatic episode can be comfortably fitted into any television news broadcast, precisely as intended.

"A Female Voice"?

The most prominent common denominator for all the above-described events is that of their "didactic" nature determined by the perspective of religious-Zionism. Plato's conception of art, which permits only "mediocre" and instrumental art (while rejecting "art for art's sake") is at the centre of such theatre, whose purpose is to serve political ends, both internal and external.

---

[32] Martin Esslin, "Reality into Fiction", *The Age of Television*, San Francisco, W.H. Freeman and Co., 1982, 57–74.

These performances are created by women who function to "mediate" between the secular and religious worlds. Some of them are *baalot teshuva* [members of a group of secular Jews who have converted to Orthodox Judaism], including over half the actresses in *Mirkam*, and who possibly bring with them from their secular past a greater daring, that eases their appearance on a public stage. Others, such as Zippora Luria and Nadia Matar, are *shomrot mitzvot* ["observe the command-ments"] but not Orthodox – an intermediate situation, which also smooths their way to dealing with secular methods and materials and using them for the requirements of the religious-Zionist audience. The stand-up comedy performers too serve as "mediators" due to their secu-lar training and their skill in this profession, so novel to their particular audience.

The experimental nature of this theatre should not be mistaken, despite its adoption of the rhetorical conventions of the fringe theatre. Conventions that do not imitate reality, as can be learned from the theatrical approach of Bertolt Brecht, are the more suitable to emphasize contents and ideas. In the religious women's theatre, these contents sanctify the religious tradition in its religious-Zionist version.

The choice of particular rhetorical conventions is matched to the actresses and their target audiences. The women's community theatre of Samaria thus deliberately copies stage conventions from the kibbutz fes-tival tradition which thereby serve as an ideological statement, making it a "natural" continuation to the (secular!) pioneering tradition. A festival, which does not require professional experience, is therefore suitable for amateur theatre. The choice of stand-up comedy is in itself a political act, and the very fact of it being presented by women constitutes a sort of attempt to shatter the stereotypes held by the secular (to whom this genre usually belongs) regarding religious-Zionist society. Stand-up comedy nonetheless demands talent and experience and is highly suited to these two professional actresses. Street theatre, which is generally used to serve "radical" goals (left-wing in the Israeli political jargon) has succeeded by means of the media in reaching wide audiences, due to the interesting contrast that it makes between a novel structure and its contents, which are the opposite of radical (or right-wing according to the jargon). From a professional point of view, with the exception of Nadia Matar's audacity, none of the participants are trained; quite the opposite – they are largely rank amateurs and the declamatory texts with the masks and puppets are compatible with their limited abilities.

The subtext of all these performances reveals a great deal about the change in women's status within a religious-Zionist group. The male system (the rabbis) which authorizes such performances, and which also supports them (community centres and the Samaria–Judea council), may not yet have fully grasped their *internal* potential for change – the possibility for women to make their voices heard in public places and by means of the media. Has "the genie got out of the bottle?" Will these women now also use their permitted theatrical activities when their group is in distress, as a lever to improve their social status? This possibility is already showing signs within the performances themselves, as well as in their reception by the female religious audience. These are in any case questions about a *possibility*, whose realisation belongs to the future.

5

THE THEATRICAL BATTLE FOR
THE SOULS OF BELIEVERS

Baalei teshuva [those who repent and atone for their sins and return to full observance of Jewish law], the newly converted to Orthodoxy and ultra-Orthodoxy, like the religious who become secular, are "in-between" individuals from both sides of a deep schism in Israeli society. The complex and antagonistic relationship between the secular and the religious in Israel has provided an important role for theatre practitioners. These have variously placed their artistic talents either at the service of religion or against those who have "returned to the religious fold".

The religious community (the ultra-Orthodox and the Zionist), living among a secular majority, has in the last decade begun to direct some of its own into the "media business" with the aid of the *baalei teshuva* and to create dramatic texts, mainly for television. Their main aims are practical: election propaganda, and video or audio recorded sermons, both for internal reinforcement among the community of believers and to present their viewpoints to the external secular community. The religious camp aims its words directly against the hegemonic group in Israeli society, with its preferential status in Israeli culture, and particularly against what it calls "the threshold guardians" – the secular leaders and the media which they believe to be controlled by a secular-*Ashkenazi* [Jews of European origin] elite to serve its own needs.[1] The theatrical-religious sermons are directed in the main to an audience of oriental origin, characterized by economic and social inferiority. The rabbis/preachers exploit the sense of frustration felt by their audience and attack the secular intelligentsia, the politicians, the media and the judiciary. They announce the failure of the Enlightenment movement [the *Haskalah*] to achieve its prediction of a Judaism without religion, and proclaim the evil of the Zionist dream in creating a secular Jewish State – an absolute oxymoron from their point of view.

The secular theatre, for its part, is attracted to the subject of conversion to ultra-Orthodoxy by its strangeness, and the sense of threat that it arouses among the secular audience. Proselytization is presented by the secular theatre in a negative light, to no small extent because of its

---

[1] Tamar El-Or, "*Tinokot she'nishbu*, Perception of Secularity among the ultra-Orthodox", *Megemot*, Vol. 34, No. 1, 1991, particularly 113–6. (Hebrew)

success in attracting youth – many of whom are the children of upper middle class parents of western origin.[2] The *baal teshuva* is characterized as one who is motivated by a sense of alienation towards the values of the society in which he lives;[3] his actions are thus also interpreted as harmful to the Zionist "civil religion" and the secular culture, and as a harsh criticism of this way of life. This situation makes demands upon the theatre, which is perceived by its audience as a sort of "secular synagogue" and which airs the various problems of concern to its audience.

Teshuva [the return to total observance of the Jewish Law] finds theatrical expression not only in the established theatre but also throughout the entire theatrical "field". Any discussion of the subject cannot therefore restrict itself solely to theatre texts but must also examine other aspects, such as actors, entertainers, directors and playwrights.

Actors

Theatre artists, particularly actors, have a special place in Israeli society. They are perceived as "Bohemians"; as a group of celebrities, much talked about, who behave according to their own liberal code. Their "flamboyant" lifestyles occasionally supply material for newspaper gossip columns and they are depicted as the most secular of all – radical apostates – who repudiate all religion, including the "civil religion". Clearly this image does not provide an accurate reflection of all actors, but there does appear to be a mitigating tendency towards tolerance by many people, who regard actors as an exception to the generally agreed rules of morality, and even accept their transgression of the law. Hanna Rovina, "mother" of the Israeli theatre, was both an unmarried mother and the quite separate partner of a hard-drinking Bohemian poet. In the puritanical atmosphere of the 1930s, this provided an unending source of popular conversation: "what no-one would have stood for from any other woman, they were ready to lovingly accept from Rovina."[4] A later example of this lenient attitude to theatre practitioners is that of Uri Zohar, the noted actor, director and entertainer, who was tried for drug-related offences in the 1970s, and whom we shall discuss later in detail. His behaviour in court was relaxed and even jocular and the press gave him favourable coverage.

Because of this image of a "free life-style", unfettered by the accepted norms and moral code, actors who make the transition from

---

[2] Yehudith El-Dor, *Types of Perspective and Attitudes regarding Teshuva among High School Students*, M.A. Thesis, Tel Aviv University, 1985. (Hebrew)

[3] Shaul Meizlish, *Return to Judaism*, Givatayim, Masada, 1984 (Hebrew); Janet Aviad, *Return to Judaism, a Religious Renewal in Israel*, Chicago and London, The University of Chicago Press, 1983.

[4] Carmit Gai, *Hanna Rovina*, Tel Aviv, Am Oved, 1995, 186. (Hebrew)

secularity to keeping the religious commandments tend to shock the secular community and arouse their curiosity. The most prominent of such "transitional" figures is Uri Zohar, who in his time managed to create for himself (in both his films and reality) the image of "an aging Peter Pan".[5] Zohar's transition to the "other" world, in the mid 1980s, still provides a source of interest and amazement, anxiety and outright hostility. The writer and journalist Didi Menussi's reaction is typical: "Uri Zohar was my friend 25 years ago, and I'll never forget what he did to me. War has two situations: one, that you become a deserter; but that's nothing compared to a situation in which you become a traitor."[6]

The acting profession, and the sensitivity it demands, lends the actors an openness to taking upon themselves other identities as a way of life. One can distinguish between two groups of actors: those who preserve their own identity while being able to adopt others on stage; and those who can only act and are according to Donald Winnicott, "completely at a loss when not in a role, and when not appreciated or applauded (acknowledged as existing)".[7] Actors live under constant stress. They must carry out their "mission" successfully while being totally exposed on stage to the audience. Their future is uncertain and the majority have no permanent job. This combination of insecurity and freedom of expression leads actors to situations of extremes. Those of them who seek a stable framework as a solution may reach religion, which offers them peace of mind, security and also "a substitute parent".[8] This may be a partial or full explanation for the *teshuva* of several well-known actors: in the 1980s – Uri Zohar, Ika Israeli, Mordechai ("Pupik") Arnon; in the 1990s – Irit Sheleg, Shuli Rand, Iris Borer, Shmuel Vilozny and Yehuda Barkan.

The *trajectoire* of Irit Sheleg was meteoric.[9] In 1981, upon completing her studies at the age of 22, she was offered the role of Desdemona by the Cameri theatre, a period during which most young actors advanced only very slowly. The press treated her with admiration, also noting her outstanding beauty as a possible reason for her success. To the surprise of many she abandoned the "safety", as she saw it, of mainstream theatre, for commercial theatre ("in commercial theatre I compete

---

[5] Renan Shor, "Aging Children", *Kolnoa* 75, April–May 1975, 4–17. (Hebrew)

[6] Yirmy Amir, "Every Morning I connect with the *Tefillin* [phylacteries] to the Most Holy Blessed be He", *Yediot Aharonot, 7 Yamim*, 1 March 1996. (Hebrew)

[7] D. W. Winnicott, "Ego Distortion in Terms of True and False Self", *The Maturational Processes and the Facilitating Environment: Studies in the Theory of Emotional Development*, London, Karnak Books, 1990, 150.

[8] Antti Oksanen, *Religious Conversion, A Meta-Analytical Study*, Lund, Lund University Press, 1994, 29–30.

[9] I use the term *trajectoire* as distinct from biography, in the meaning given by Pierre Bourdieu. *Les Règles de l'art*, Paris, Seuil, 1992, 359–63.

for every ticket")[10]. She also gained experience in alternative fringe theatre, took part in several films, and in one of them (*Not for Broadcasting*,
directed by Yaud Lebanon, 1981) she appeared in the nude. Within the
theatre Sheleg was perceived as "unstable", living in a state of constant
unease, which progressively worsened, eventually leading to her abandoning her acting career.[11]

Irit Sheleg attempts to explain the change in direction, her conversion to ultra-Orthodoxy, as beginning with her childhood. She describes
her secular life as "beautiful and successful," [but] "in spite of that I felt a
great emptiness and dissatisfaction inside, a constant hunger, and then
you begin to ask questions." She relates to her childhood in several
respects: "I grew up in a home without boundaries. Under such circumstances everything boils over. So you look for a lid." She mentions
a grandfather who for a long period provided a father figure for her and
with whom she lived. Sheleg's memories of childhood provide some
explanation for her *teshuva*: "I think that it began at an early age.
I remember myself playing truant from school and going to the beach.
Sitting on the shore facing the open sea and beginning to feel a sense
of yearning. And asking myself what I was yearning for." She continues:
"I always remember myself as preoccupied with longings."[12] Sheleg,
who grew up "in a house in which Judaism did not exist," began to
study Judaism during her search for the meaning of longings in other
areas – psychology, philosophy, the wisdom of the East. She connects the
actual turnabout to a rabbi she met whose words affected her deeply and
touched her heart. Listening to him aroused the same sense of yearning
within her that she had experienced in her childhood:

> I remember the day [...] I remember that moment [...] I looked at the man
> and dropped my glance. *Awed for the first time in my life* (emphasis mine,
> D.U.). He began to talk and he spoke and spoke... he spoke about the

---

[10] From my interview with Irit Sheleg on 9 January 1996. All further quotations are taken
from the same interview.

[11] Amalia Argaman-Barnea, "Returning to Herself", *Yediot Aharonot*, 3 August 1988.
(Hebrew)

[12] The decisive role played by parents in their children's tending toward religion can be
learned from the actor Shuli Rand. Rand was born into a religious home and at a very young
age became secular, following two family tragedies: his older brother died and shortly afterwards a sister was born with Down's Syndrome. His parents explained these tragedies to
him, according to their religious reasoning, as God taking back for himself the good children. Shuli Rand, the child who feared that God would take him too, began secretly to avoid
carrying out the religious commandments, removing his skullcap, turning on the lights on
the Sabbath – until reaching secularity. He is currently undergoing religious conversion,
which he explains as a return to those sources to which he belongs; from an interview with
Cobi Midan, "Nocturnal Meeting", *Israeli Television*, Channel 2, 30 January 1996.

immanence of the Torah. I didn't understand a single word he said, but my soul must have understood every word. I simply felt that I was sitting there when suddenly a tap was turned on within me and I was crying and crying. Without knowing why I was crying. I wanted time to stand still and for me to go on listening to the rabbi. Those same *yearnings* (D.U.) that I used to feel as a child on the seashore, I felt at that very moment.

Sheleg's description is similar to many other descriptions of situations in which, for similar reasons, a return to the religious fold is expedited by means of a key figure – a chosen agent – who may "replace" the real parents. John Bowlby speaks of the "attachment figure" as one's trusted companion:

> Human beings of all ages are happiest and able to deploy their talents to best advantage, when they are confident that, standing behind them, there are one or more trusted persons who will come to their aid should difficulties arise. The person trusted, also known as an attachment figure, can be considered as providing his (or her) companion with a secure base from which to operate.[13]

This attachment figure can be God himself (substituting for a father figure or a mother figure), but also an "intermediary" figure – a preacher, priest, rabbi – who demonstrates by his faith the "higher ideal in life."[14] Uri Zohar describes such an attachment figure: "This Jew to whom I owe my life", as an important figure in the change he underwent.[15] Yehuda Barkan, entertainer, actor and director, who was particularly famous for his candid camera films, which included pornographic scenes, also arrived at a stage of (partial) *teshuva* through the influence of the rabbis.[16]

Teshuva provides the actor with a protective environment, like a family, possibly as an answer to unsatisfied childhood needs, and particularly to a lifestyle devoid of any security. To supply these needs, shared by many secularists, the proselytizers employ the texts of their theatrical homilies and sermons as a strategy aimed at such "conversions".

---

[13] John Bowlby, *Making and Breaking of Affectional Bonds*, London, Tavistock Publications, 1979, 103.

[14] Research by Antti Oksanen into religious conversion has revealed hundreds of such cases linked to the John Bowlby attachment theory. A key figure in the process of religious conversion according to Oksanen is "the attachment figure" who may "replace" the parents. According to this theory, individuals of any age are happier and better able to utilise their talents if they believe that another (or several other) figures will come to their help in times of difficulty. Note 8, 129–58.

[15] From an interview with Yael Dan, "Personal Story", *Israeli Television*, Channel 1, 5 May 1996.

[16] Amir, note 6.

The Dramatic Marketing of *Teshuva*

Proselytizers include among their persuasive techniques those of a dramatic nature.[17] In addition to booklets, posters and cassettes, they hold meetings in peoples' homes and give seminars and sermons to large audiences before which the most famous *baalei teshuva* appear, such as Uri Zohar, or the seekers of a Jewish way of life, such as Yehuda Barkan, who provide personal examples of a successful path. The actors appear in "uniform", attesting to their choice – the full ultra-Orthodox garb in Zohar's case; beard, white skullcap and *tefillin* [phylacteries] for Barkan – publicly demonstrating their faith in their new path. "Until today I was an actor, far from the Most Holy, blessed be He. Today I am an actor who believes in the Most Holy, and in the Creator of the Universe," stated Barkan at one such gathering.[18] The choice of actor for such gatherings is frequently made according to the principle of casting a celebrity for a theatre play.[19]

The majority of the texts used by the proselytizers set out from a standpoint close to that of their addressees and thus use the semiotic vocabulary and concepts of their audience. They organise group simulation games, a distinctly dramatic activity, during which the rabbis, lecturers and other team members play secular roles, while the secular participants represent the religious factor. The temporarily "secular" rabbi tries to "persuade" the genuinely secular person who is playing a religious role, that it is permitted to travel on the Sabbath, while the secular person in his new role must marshal his arguments to the defence of religion. After all have reverted to their own identities, the path to persuasion is far easier.[20]

During such games the secular identity adopted by the proselytizer is generally one which does not disguise his religiosity. He may also play the role of a dramatic figure, adopting more sophisticated theatrical techniques.[21] Rabbi Benji Levene, for example, from the "Gesher" [bridge]

---

[17] On the uses of advanced modern technologies for reinforcing traditional religious values, see: David Chaney, *Fictions of Collective Life*, London and New York, Routledge, 1993, 177. See also reference by Ali Yassif to audio and video tapes as "an example of proselytization strategy: using recognised symbols from the secular world – radio and television – in order to bring about their destruction." Ali Yassif, "Tales of Religious Conversion: Rhetoric, Folklore and Ideology in Israeli Reality", *Pages for Literary Research*, 9, 1993–4, 128. (Hebrew) He goes on to study "Dramatic-theatrical techniques" of one of the proselytizers, 142.

[18] Amir, note 6.

[19] Michael Quinn claims that "there is something in the dramatic performance that causes the spectator to seek information about the personal life of the actor and to store this 'life' in a celebrity box." Moreover, the famous figure, the celebrity, may be an agent for the strategy of a certain ideological approach, see M. L. Quinn, "Celebrity and the Semiotics of Acting", *New Theatre Quarterly*, 22, May 1990, 154–61.

[20] Meizlish, note 3, 160.

[21] Yassif, note 17.

organisation, has been appearing in the play *The Four Faces of Israel* since 1978. He plays and manipulates fictitious characters before a mixed secular and religious audience. The play is didactic, of a comic-educational nature ("An Educational Comedy of Jewish Identity"). It is followed by discussion groups led by instructors. Rabbi Levene rationalises the problematic and even forbidden choice (from the point of view of religious law) of the theatre medium, by his desire to introduce serious questions relating to the essence of the Jewish identity and to guide the spectators into considering and clarifying their viewpoints. He does not "seek a comic performance."[22] The contradiction in his approach, between his "theatrical approach" and his aim of proselytization, demonstrates the tension between the religious message and the theatrical frame associated with secularism.

Levene is not a self-declared proselytizer. He defines his activities and his organisation as aimed at slowing down assimilation and as a barrier against "corrupt western culture."[23] While the play has no explicit appeal for *teshuva*, its aims are not far from those of a gathering directly intended as such. His comedy creates a renewed hierarchy of archetypes representing different value perspectives in Jewish Israeli society. The four figures in the play are: an elderly ultra-Orthodox man from Mea Shearim [an ultra-Orthodox neighbourhood in Jerusalem]; a bus driver (representing the middle and lower class secular Israeli); an American tourist from the Jewish National Fund; and an assimilated Jewish artist of French origin living in Zefat and married to a Christian woman. The emphasis is on the positive nature of the religious figure and the ridiculous and lost nature of the other three. The play helps its religious audience to reinforce their directed beliefs, and its secular audience towards a "soft" *teshuva*.

The play evolves as a series of interviews. One of the (female) instructors interviews Rabbi Levene in his four different roles. The order of appearance of the characters is significant. The first figure, presented in a positive light, is that of the ultra-Orthodox Jew; he is followed by the secular figures who represent disappointing alternatives.

The most problematic character from Levene's point of view is that of Jean-Paul Simon, the assimilated artist, because secular youth tend to identify with him. Levene accordingly frequently eliminates him from the performance. Jean-Paul offers a world vision that is cosmopolitan, anti-religious, peace-loving, caring for all mankind – characteristics more likely to attract sympathy than to repulse. For Levene this is a threatening and

---

[22] From an interview in the *Jerusalem Post*, 30 December 1988. Meizlish, a supporter of *teshuva*, includes the "Gesher" organisation among the proselytizing bodies, see Meizlish, note 3, 26, 148.

[23] From the program notes to Levene's show *The Four Faces of Israel*.

frustrating character; a monster he himself has created. Levene succeeds in "reducing" the artist by presenting him as someone who creates confused, unintelligible paintings, and who wears unusual attire – beret, socks with holes, a flamboyant belt.

The self-censorship reveals the difficulty faced by religious preachers when using dramatic techniques. These, by their very nature, are open to different readings and different audiences may interpret them in a different way to that intended by the author; a deviation which may impede their effective instrumental use. It is thus possible that the videocassettes made by the proselytes, such as those in which Uri Zohar attacks the "free" world vision, may be perceived by their secular spectators as simply an entertaining curiosity, as inarticulate texts, or even as a threat. They may, therefore, actually reinforce the secular and anti-religious viewpoint.

Ideological Conflict

Religious Jewish groups generally take a negative attitude to the theatre, neither making nor watching theatre unless for a "didactic" or political purpose. Uri Zohar relates to his artistic past as an unnecessary mistake:

> The spectator sees on the stage that for others too life is full of contradictions and lack of meaning, and he leaves satisfied. This identification and release finds its expression – on another level – also on the football field or in a pornographic magazine. Shakespeare only adds philosophy, ideas and emotions. This approach is clearly anti-Torah and I will therefore not support it. Not as a spectator and not as a creative artist. The Torah deals with quite the opposite: man must discard the trivial and unessential and concentrate only on himself.[24]

Uri Zohar at first related sceptically to the possibility that he might harness his acting and directing talents for religious ends, through fear that he might not have an audience. His approach later changed and he currently makes frequent public appearances, mostly of a theatrical nature. His public sermons are recorded and edited on tape (audio and video) and he uses them to disseminate matters of *teshuva*. In contrast and opposition to such sermons, the secular theatre has staged various plays: *Trumpeldor 85* (1985) by Shimon Zimmer; *The Last Secularist* (1986) by Shmuel Hasfari; *In Reverse* (1986) by B. Michael (a religious journalist whose play is a sort of "deconstruction" of a *teshuva* discourse); and *Bidur k'Halacha* (1994), a stand-up comedy show which

---

[24] Meizlish, note 3, 47–48.

includes a critical attitude to religious conversion, performed by two young religious-Zionist women. These plays reveal the objections raised to such conversions among both the secular and the religious-Zionist groups.

As an entertainer, Uri Zohar won great acclaim, more for his acting talent than for his humorous material. "Uri Zohar," wrote Yeshayahu Ben-Porat, "with his personal charm, his talent for acting and mimicry – is able to transmit across the stage even corny old jokes […] and he has the ability, as an individual, to elicit not only waves of laughter and thunderous applause, but something far more important and rare: a good mood and a tolerant one."[25] As a preacher too, Zohar does not excel in interesting texts. "His sermons are full of outworn clichés," noted the religious writer Chaim Beer.[26] Zohar himself is aware of the effect of the publicity from his past. In his homilies, as in his films, he interweaves his own image into the text. The subject matter of his films deals with biographical occurrences contemporary to the time of each film.[27] Among those who watch his video *The Birth Pangs of Redemption*, and see Rabbi Uri Zohar garbed and hatted in black, there are probably many who recognise the actor Uri Zohar, whose films are still frequently screened, displaying a naked upper torso, short pants and outrageous tricks. Zohar uses this tension between then and now, between the past "sinner" whose pleasure seeking and flippancy are well documented, and the body language and rhetoric of an angry prophet publicly reproaching the sinful.

Most of the videotape of *The Birth Pangs of Redemption*[28] is taken up with Uri Zohar's appearance before an audience. He uses this appearance to appeal to two types of spectator – those in the auditorium and those watching the tape at home. The laughter and applause were edited onto the tape later. The accepted practice when filming a speech is usually to provide a view of the assembled audience. For the tape in question, however, the particular audience was not filmed in order to "broaden" Zohar's appeal to a far wider audience.

The contents are directed at a working class audience of oriental origin. It is important to note in this connection that the secular Uri Zohar had been one of the most prominent representatives of that same elite *Ashkenazi* culture that had suppressed, according to his present version of events, those from an oriental background. From the first moment,

---

[25] Yeshayahu Ben-Porat, "Uri Zohar Vilified Me and Enchanted Me", *La'Isha*, 25 June 1963. (Hebrew)

[26] Chaim Beer, "Local hero", *Davar*, 2 December 1983. (Hebrew)

[27] Renan Shor, "The Cinematic Experience – the *Tsabar* Image in Uri Zohar's Films", *Kolnoa 78*, No. 15–16, 1978, 41. (Hebrew)

[28] My students Lenny Shahaf and Erez Gottlieb of the Theatre Department of Tel Aviv University introduced me to the tape. Some of the analytic elements are taken from work carried out by them under my instruction.

Zohar preaches that we "are living in terrible times" caused by the poisoning of souls by the "guardians of the threshold". The source of all evil as pinpointed by all these homilies, is those secular *Ashkenazis* who are ashamed of their Jewishness; they and their failed Zionist religion, which is a later development of the Jewish Enlightenment. This dangerous situation will lead to assimilation and to destruction. However, there is a solution: *Teshuva*, which will also lead to redemption.

One of the secular theatre's first reactions to the proselytic activity could be seen in *Trumpeldor 85* (1985) by Shimon Zimmer, directed by Yossef Karmon. In this satire the Minister of Defence appears at the home of a family who lost their son in the Yom Kippur War (1973); he bemoans his troubles: a new war is about to break out and he doesn't have enough soldiers. The few who are left no longer have any ideals. He proposes to restore their son to life for one night, on condition that the following day the son will be prepared to set off once more for war "with his former ideals". The parents consent to the proposal and the son agrees to die once more. One of the characters in the play is a proselytizer who attempts to persuade the son to enter a *yeshiva* [college of Torah study] instead of re-enlisting in the army; to choose Judaism over fulfilling the commands of the Zionist "civil religion". His speech is a parody of one of Uri Zohar's sermons:

> Shalom Jewish sinners … shalom to the many sons with their parents … the many parents with their sons … shalom to a neighbourhood of sin … to those fed up with hearing lectures on acupuncture … to those fed up with hearing about the hemispheres and meditation … to those fed up with hearing about the holistic approach to healing chronic illness, to those fed up with hearing about herpes … come, approach me, ye holy flock [...] come and listen to me ye misguided souls … I too was a secular pig … I too was in the pit of sin and drugs … I too smoked the sweet weed … I too spilled my hot seed on vile pictures … O God … you have forsaken us. Abandoned in the rain [...] I close my eyes … and there is America … on the shores of the Mississippi … with greying beard – stands Herzl … the man who dreamed us … the man who stood 100 years ago on the banks of the river in Vienna … I look at him and his eyes touch mine … and in his hand the broken Zionist dream … assimilation … and where he wished to take us before it all began … to Uganda … yes, to be Negroes … [29]

The new religiosity of conversion to ultra-Orthodoxy was written about by B. Michael (a religious journalist who lived among secular

---

[29] Herzl did indeed consider Uganda as a temporary solution, after failing in his efforts to achieve a charter for the Land of Israel from the Turkish sultan. The proposal was shelved after his death.

Jews), in a play aimed at "revealing" the manipulation and ignorance of those with pretensions to "knowing the right path". *In Reverse* (1986) is an anti-sermon or stand-up comedy that mocks religious conversion, its arguments and the jargon of its emissaries and followers.

The proselytizer in the play is depicted as "a magician who performs his magic tricks, but immediately reveals how he does them."[30] The character refers to Uri Zohar, and to quotes from interviews with him. Zohar's mention of his secular past: "I was okay, just as Adam and Eve were okay before they tasted the apple,"[31] is developed in the play into a speech:

> Tell me about drugs! I was there. Tell me about lechery! I was there. Tell me about profligacy, money, entertainment, alcohol, tomfoolery, publicity, high society – all those wonderful things that it takes to fill your lives nowadays – I was there! I've tasted that poison! You can't teach me anything new! And only now, from the place I'm at right now, can I see all these things in the right perspective: all is vanity! Folly! Misery! All the parties in the world, and all the money, and all the material pleasure that exists – are not worth even half of one Sabbath spent according to *halacha* in a Jewish house. That is true happiness. Perfect. Complete.

The methods used by the proselytizers are shown up by B. Michael, who critically breaks down the "logic" of one of Zohar's sermons:

> Perhaps you know Rabbi Uri Zohar – one of our great proselytizers. In an interview he once gave he said that the proof, which I shall now present to you, is one of the principal proofs which led to his own *teshuva*. It goes like this: In *Leviticus* Ch. 11 the Bible enumerates those animals which it is permitted to eat and those which are forbidden [...]. It is permitted to eat those which chew the cud and have cloven hoofs and forbidden to eat those which do not. These are things which even you know. Now, something interesting occurs there: the Bible determines that in all the world there are only three animals which chew the cud but do not have cloven hoofs: the camel, the coney and the hare [...] So can you explain to me how Moses could establish this with such certainty? [...] Only one being could provide such a guarantee: a superhuman being – the Creator of the World.

> It's true – there is a small problem here; the coney and hare do not chew the cud [...] so could it be possible that the Torah is mistaken? That Uri

---

[30] From an interview with my student Osnat Ganor.
[31] Meizlish, note 3, 44.

Zohar is mistaken? No! The coney and the hare are mistaken! They're simply felons.

The ending to *In Reverse* reveals conversion to ultra-Orthodoxy as a self-contradictory phenomenon and presents its messages as false:

> If you simply remember what we have learned here today – that coercion – is love. A secularist – is a coward. Freedom – is rubbish. Science – is nonsense. Progress – is regression. Forward – is backward. And the main thing – there is only an answer where there are no questions – if you remember all that – I can relax. You, *all of you* [emphasis in original], will eventually reach us …

In Reverse attempts to reveal the "pseudo-intellect" and "pseudo-logic" employed by the proselytizers through their distortion of facts, misquotations and deliberately forced *gimatria* [a form of numerology] games. Exposure of this deception reinforces the secular audience's objections; an audience which is well aware that efforts at *teshuva* are being directed at it and its values, and which fears the possible effect. For this audience, plays that ridicule religious conversion constitute a sort of exorcism ritual. Such a ritual can be found in the pointed satire by Shmuel Hasfari, *The Last Secularist* (1986), directed by the playwright at the Cameri Theatre. The events take place in an ultra-Orthodox State founded upon the ruins of the secular State of Israel. One of the scenes features a proselyte, a former entertainer, who needs to "repent his dubious past" and who must "turn a new page in a new artistic career" by farting the tune of "Hatikva", the anthem of the Zionist State. Chupchik, the entertainer, has difficulty in producing farts. In order to help him the ultra-Orthodox employ Pavlovian stimuli: they show him the flag of Israel and sound the siren for Remembrance Day.[32]

The ultra-Orthodox group has its own reservations regarding the *baalei teshuva*, and its attitude towards them is discriminatory.[33] A similar attitude, albeit more moderate, is shown by the religious Zionists.[34] One expression of this can be found in a stand-up comedy performance by two young religious women, Noya Shuster and Nurit Hadar, graduates of the Bnei Akiva religious youth movement, religious

---

[32] This scene aroused a stormy public debate; it was also censored. The official Board of Censors for Film and Theatre, which initially banned the entire play, eventually restricted itself to eliminating certain scenes including the above. The Board was convinced that the play "greatly damages the basic values and feelings of a wide section of the public, both religious and secular," and is "an inciting satire that may stir up hatred." *Davar*, 1 December 1986.

[33] El-Or, note 1, 118–9.

[34] Meizlish, note 3, 168–9.

schooling and army service. They are exceptional in having undertaken graduate theatre studies and in performing before mixed audiences in stand-up comedy – a "secular-yuppie" genre. While the actresses them-selves serve as "intermediaries", thanks to their secular training and skill in this new (for the religiously observant) profession, they also take care to express their reservations regarding the *baalei teshuva*. Noya Shuster criticizes the religious conversion of the oriental Jews which, as she sees it, involves a "payment", and finds even greater fault with the proselytiz-ers. Her opinion on the subject of Uri Zohar is explicit: she sees him as a former secularist who following "conversion" is now convinced that only he possesses the key to truth.[35] The two women present the entire attempt at proselytism as ridiculous and false, with one of them speaking as a *baal teshuva*:

> Lord, Lord of … what's that? You've moved to here? You've been discov-ered by fans, they've come to ask for your autograph? Right. It really is better here. Fresh air, scenery … Lord, is it alright for me to talk to you like this? After all, I've been a *baal teshuva* for one week […] but there are two sides to this two-way route. I've done my share, and you – what? Hear O Israel … that's your name isn't it? Okay, you don't need to get upset, we've known each other for a week! Take care of the matter for me and I'll carry out the commandments for you, you've never seen any-thing like it … the Ten Commandments? Big deal! Honour thy father – honoured. I'll honour my mother too. Thou shalt not kill – won't kill. Thou shalt not steal – I'll try … Thou shalt not commit adultery – I haven't adulterated … with the neighbour's wife it's not adultery. Listen, your writing's not too clear! Okay, this evening for the last time. So what's to become of me? What shall I do? … To come to you? No, thank you, no, no, I like to be close to earth, and I'm also afraid of heights.

The play was performed many times before religious-Zionist audiences who, according to the two actresses, did not appear to have any reservations about the monologue. The rabbis too, who gave their blessing for the show, did not demand any form of censorship, which is informative regarding the suspicions and double-standard approach of the religious audience to the *baal teshuva* and his motives.

Semiotic Conflict: Language, Body Language, Costume, Place and Accessories

The proselyte alters his language, clothing and habits, and a change also takes places in his personal standards and values. Accommodating to a

---

[35] From an interview with Noya Shuster.

new language reflects "a deeper process of socialization".[36] It constitutes an important element in the ideo-semiotic conflict between the two camps, also noticeable in their changed attitude to the body and in an altered use of body language, clothing and other accessories.

Uri Zohar displays a diminishing awareness of the type of style required to create a link with the audience, and perhaps also a diminished sense of value regarding one important achievement of Zionism – rebirth of the Hebrew language. There is a certain degree of protest in the choice of language used by the proselytes, particularly in the adoption of Yiddish, or the deliberately incorrect use of language. Nissim Yagen, a proselytizing performer, tends toward "sub-standard Hebrew [...] he deliberately uses expressions and a vocabulary or broken language [...] that speak to the less educated stratum of the population."[37] This is also the style used by Rabbi Amnon Yitzhak, who is also a proselytizer: "When I was in a secular school, the biology teacher told me that my ancestors were apes. *Inteh wa abuk* (Arabic: you and your father) are monkeys, I told him (audience laughs). Then he showed me drawings of how such a little monkey becomes a lawyer (laughter). The next day the Bible teacher told me that God created us. I told him: Just a moment, yesterday the biology teacher said that I came from an ape, who is right? Free choice, he told me. Okay, I understood. But during recess where do we play – on the ground or on the trees? (the audience is rocking in the aisles)."[38] In the secular plays, this mixture of styles and languages is used to depict the proselytizer as ridiculous and a cheat. The jargon that Yehoshua Sobol places in the mouth of the eponymous "hero" in his translation of *Tartuffe*, is that used by the proselytizers. The change of language and its fluctuations, the mixture of high and low styles, and religious and secular vocabularies, creates a new and self-contradictory language.

Tartuffe by Molière, staged by the Haifa Municipal Theatre (1985) was translated by Sobol into the language of proselytism during a period which witnessed the height of this phenomenon in Israel. The translator's overt attack on the proselytizers was "served up" in Cleante's speech (*Tartuffe* I, 5):

> These people who with the fervour of *hypocritical messianity* [translator's addition, D.U.] rush around/to make a fortune, please God, and don't forget to demand/their pleasures between their prayers [...]/ These people who know how to suit their religion to their needs and desires,

---

[36] Mordechai Rottenberg, *Seventy Faces of Life, a Sermonizing Biography as Personal Psychotherapy*, trans. by Yitzhak Komem, Jerusalem, Bialik Institute, 1994, 205. (Hebrew)
[37] Yassif, note 17, 142.
[38] Gai Ben-Porat, "He Takes their Children", *Ha'Ir*, 3 May 1996.

these are the scoundrels, the bearers of grudges, the peddlers of faith, the plotters/ In their bitterness and wrath they endanger humanity/ for no weapon sickens them/ including the cynical use of the religious feelings of the people/ and so they murder the soul of mankind in the most methodical way/ *Recently* (emphasis mine, D.U.) the counterfeit types have become increasingly common.[39]

"If one chooses to stage *Tartuffe* today," explains Sobol, "it is because life in Israel is in the grip of madness, of religious sanctimoniousness and hypocrisy." Regarding language, he notes: "In translating, I set out from this reality and go towards Molière, with my ears echoing with the language of Shapira, Goren and Porush [noted rabbis and religious politicians in the 1980s]: '*kashrut* supervisors', 'sacrificial hen', 'God be blessed', etc. Tartuffe interests me as a proselytizer, as a candidate for the Rabbinate, as a rabbi."[40] Orgon, as a *baal teshuva*, in Sobol's version, adopts the language of the ultra-Orthodox, employing such expressions as "a blessing for every deed", "he has a watchful, wary and ultra-Orthodox eye", "blessed be the Lord", "as God wills", etc. This satiric depiction of Tartuffe reached its heights in the play in the courtship of Elmire. Tartuffe undresses before having intercourse with the wife of his friend, a pious man, and remains on stage with only his loins barely covered – and a skullcap on his head. In order to seduce Elmire into believing that they are not breaking any religious law, he tells her (in the Hebrew version): "If you will become *teshuva*, I'll introduce you to the orchards of the Jewish law. I'll lead you by degrees to the practice and reveal to you the secret – if you only let me guide you in the way of the flesh." (*ibid.* 80–81)

At the close of the 20th century, which worships the body, it is the spirit or soul which presents a problem for the body,[41] in contrast to both Christian and Jewish religious concepts, which perceive the body as a restricting obstacle, a confining vessel whose desires must be overcome.[42] The contrasting perceptions of the body by the secular and the religious are featured in *Boochie* (1984) by Yossef Bar-Yossef, staged at the Haifa Municipal Theatre under the direction of Gedalia Besser, adapted

---

[39] Molière, *Tartuffe*, Hebrew version: Yehoshua Sobol, Tel Aviv, Or-Am, 1985, 21. Sobol retained Moliere's text for the major part, only altering a few details. Nonetheless, the translation is in the main Jewish-Israeli and "equivalent" expressions to the French change their meaning and anchor the play in its Israeli connection. Thus, for example, "Lately" is the translator's addition that brings the play closer to the phenomenon of *teshuva*, which reached one of its high points in the middle of the 1980s.

[40] Hanna Rosenthal, "Tartuffe as a Proselytizer", *Al Ha'Mishmar*, 21 March 1985. (Hebrew)

[41] Anthony Synnott, *The Body Social: Symbolism, Self and Society*, London and New York, Routledge, 1993, 34–6.

[42] David Biale, *Eros and the Jews*, Tel Aviv, Am Oved, 1994, 13. (Hebrew)

for television (1991) by Gilad Evron, and directed by Ram Levy. The religious characters in the play cover up their bodies and obscure their physical and sexual identities, hiding behind black suits, voluminous dresses and head coverings. Baruch (Boochie) the son, who has suddenly returned to his father's house from the outside (secular) world, to seek refuge from his creditors, uncovers the hidden physical sexuality. When Boochie sings in the shower, his ultra-Orthodox brother-in-law says of the secular: "their bodies make them happy."[43] His sister, ultra-Orthodox and married, confesses to Boochie her love for another man: "With him I feel naked," she repeats several times, raising her voice: "Naked! Naked! Naked!" And he shushes her: "Enough. Naked is only once. It's not Holy, Holy, Holy!" (*ibid.* 91) Boochie's encounter with a young ultra-Orthodox woman, who wants to cross over to secularism, almost ends in love-making. She displays her body to him, rolls down her black stockings and hikes up her dress. Boochie: "Here too they take off their clothes for me. What am I, a shower?" (94).

The first theatre text to present the feminine aspect of proselytism was *One Hundred New Apples Including VAT* (1996) by Ora Morag and Israel Gurion. It is the story of a secular woman coerced into *teshuva* by her husband. She recounts her story after separating from her husband and religious life. The play was staged by a commercial theatre with the apparent aim of pure entertainment. However, every peek by critical secular eyes into the ultra-Orthodox world heightens the conflict between the two worlds and discloses the clash of ideologies.

The play is a humorous report on the phenomenon of "following the husband's footsteps" and to a great extent also the footsteps of a tyranny which increases with proselytism. The woman is forced to adapt to a new world which condemns her. In addition to the obligation of providing a livelihood, she must also adjust to the hard labour of housework in a home which upholds all the commandments of Judaism. She must come to terms with a husband who has altered all his habits and begun to speak Yiddish. The most extreme change takes place in the attitude to the body and sex. She wears clothing that suffocates her: "I'm hot. I'm hot – inside the clothes." However, one good point that she finds in the ultra-Orthodox way of life is that the man does not need to overcome his bodily urges – his new religion does not permit him to do so: "Whoever wants to quit – please do so, there is Christianity! [...] but no need to struggle in Judaism. You must be with a woman – and lustily. The commandment says: sow thy seed and multiply and pleasure thy wife." Most of the scenes in the play disclose the sexual urges and physicality

---

[43] Yossef Bar-Yossef, *Difficult People, Four Plays*, "Boochie", Tel Aviv, Am Oved, 1986, 66. (Hebrew)

beneath the trappings of religious conversion, and the legitimization of "quickie sex". A deliberate tension is created between the constant attempt on the part of the husband and the Orthodox community to compel modesty and head to foot clothing – in one scene the husband demands that his wife wear a long skirt and not pants, returning repeatedly to button up her shirt – and between an intensive sex life on the other hand ("highly advisable for she who wants to invigorate her sex life"). The wife reiterates how she achieved a compromise with her husband over the commandment of immersion in the *mikveh* [ritual bath] – a walk to the sea and a naked dip followed by making love: "This isn't the man I married. Such a wild animal! Such urges!" Like other theatre texts, this play too deliberately exposes the physical weaknesses of those who hide beneath the trappings of religion, in order to refute the uniqueness of their beliefs.

Covering up the head and body is highly important in the ultra-Orthodox world and is featured as such on the secular stage. The *teshuva* of Boochie too in Bar-Yossef's play is accompanied by a change of clothing. In the television version, after he moves into the Orthodox neighbourhood, he begins to wear a skullcap and exchanges his jeans and red-flowered shirt for the Orthodox black garb, but with a glimpse of his former clothing still showing. In contrast to the skullcap that he puts on, his sister removes her head covering when confessing her forbidden love for another man (*ibid.* 91). Boochie, who is marking his change in identity by means of his black garb, has previously referred to the prayer-chanting, ultra-Orthodox Jews who accompany his dying father as "three stinking black coats" (*ibid.* 72). Leah, the young ultra-Orthodox girl, half questions–half determines: "You're not really going to wear this coat are you? It's just Purim? ..." (*ibid.* 93), and he avoids answering.

Body language also serves in the conflict between the two camps on the stages of both preacher and actor. The body language of Uri Zohar in the videotape *The Birth Pangs of Redemption* is characterized by a great deal of gesticulation with the hands. Movement of the body, particularly the hands and mainly the index finger, draws attention, indicating and warning. Body movements accompanying references to the secular world are filmed from a low angle. In contrast, hand gestures accompanying references to religious belief are raised high with fingers curved at head height, forming a sort of dome or roof. The gesture accompanying the words "we are with the Lord," reaches its climax with the final word, and is maintained frozen for several seconds. Zohar thus confers upon the word "Lord" an aura of tremendous protection. In the final scene of the video Zohar offers *teshuva* as a recipe for redemption and asks his listeners to take his words and make something of them. He extends the palms of his hands to his audience as if to say "take!", repeating this gesture several times, and then clenches his fists while saying "with the help of God". He ends with a gesture of throwing a ball into the audience, as if handing them God's will.

In contrast, and opposition, to Uri Zohar, the play *In Reverse* offers Alex Ansky, a well-known actor and popular radio presenter. Ansky wears for the purpose Uri Zohar's "clothes" – beard, black hat, black coat and pants and white shirt. The role necessitated the secular actor becoming acquainted with a new body language, as can be learned from a description of one of the rehearsals: "Ansky [...] wears the expression of a professorial proselytizer on his face. The face becomes as soft as jelly but eyes are burning with fire. The weight of the body is centered on the stomach. One hand strokes the beard. The change is quite startling. B. Michael, who is sitting at the side is called urgently when Ansky, out of secular bad habit, hooks a finger into the front of his trouser belt. 'Either behind your back,' corrects B. Michael, 'or on the beard.'"[44]

Desecration by Chonni Hameagel, staged at the Akko Festival of Fringe Theatre (1994), made semiotic use of the entire system of theatre signs in order to demonstrate the ridiculous nature of the *teshuva* gatherings. This was an experimental performance that critically examined religious ritual, particularly in Judaism. Prior to the performance the spectators were given two booklets: "The Modern Testament" – a collection of selected texts from the *Shulchan Aruch* [Codification of Jewish law compiled by Yossef Caro, first printed in 1565], including the rules governing the prohibition of the idle spilling of one's seed, the law of celibacy prior to a woman's menstrual period, toilet procedures and laws of atonement on the eve of Yom Kippur. In addition to the program notes, a catalogue of swimsuits by a well-known Israeli designer was also provided. Chonni Hameagel, himself from an ultra-Orthodox family, referred to the particular choice of text and audience: "Each time I try to reach that same level of banality and naivete found in the Torah. It contains so many foolish and stupid things, not to mention immoral, to the extent that I think the Torah should be made illegal. [...] The principal part of the play is the audience itself [...] I tie them to their chairs, hand out *tallithot*, burn incense, give a few pills to intoxicate them and fly them high into the air with all my music."[45]

The theatre space, a Crusader Hall, was designed as a church-cum-synagogue. The spectators were asked to remove their shoes which were collected by one of the actresses, while another actor handed out *tefillin* [phylacteries]. Both were dressed in robes reminiscent of the Hare Krishna sect. Various holy artifacts were scattered around, particularly on the dais in the front on which was set a holy ark with drawn curtains and candles, above which an illuminated sign displayed the prohibition

---

44 Michal Kafra, "Or Revers Yeshiva", *Ma'ariv*, 7 November 1987. (Hebrew)
45 *Telegraph*, Haifa and the north, Journal of the Festival, 22–23 September 1994. (Hebrew)

"Thou shalt not commit adultery". Television screens showed scenes from Uri Zohar's secular films as well as videotapes by Zohar the proselytizer. The textual blend of the sacred and the secular in *Desecration*, the range of scenes dealing with the *halachic* attitude to various personal matters, and particularly the choice of videoclips of Uri Zohar, combined to form a sort of lexicon of desecration; the complete opposite of the religious semiotic "dictionary" used by the proselytizers in their appearances. The actors read out the passages from "The Modern Testament"; actresses strode about attired in the fashionable swimsuits from the catalogue; from time to time a voice could be heard giving instructions to airline passengers; a nun passed by and stood next to the Holy Ark; the Ten Commandments were screened on an electronic board; actresses performed a striptease and one of them masturbated in front of the audience. All this was accompanied by heavy rock music. One scene that particularly focused audience attention was a "number" performed by a preacher/magician who succeeded first in pulling a dove out of the Holy Scripture and releasing it, and then slaughtered a chicken in a cruel ritual of atonement – "angering" one of the actresses who played an enraged member of the audience.

One play featuring an especially vehement objection to proselytism was *Dinner* by Amir Orian, which ran for one year (1985–6) at the Cheder (room) Theatre, to an audience numbering only 14. It was subtitled "A Lesson in *Shulchan Aruch* to an Audience of Forced Proselytes". (The Hebrew word *b'koach* [forced] in this case acquires the double meaning of possibility and coercion). In the course of the evening "the company of actors taught the audience the correct way to be good Jews."[46] According to Orian, this was an extremely difficult performance for both actors and audience, particularly the scene of ritual slaughter of the hen, which was then cooked and served to the spectators.

Amir Orian designed his play to "counterattack" Israeli culture and its theatre of the 1980s; a culture which he sees as being pseudo-religious nationalist.[47] He perceives the *teshuva* phenomenon as one indication of this trend, which during the 1980s reached a peak in the number of new *baalei teshuva*.[48] Every possible theatrical means was enlisted in his play to highlight the more repugnant elements of the religious ritual. Orian explains his approach to religion and ritual (taking in *teshuva* along

---

[46] From an interview with Amir Orian, 30 January, 1996.

[47] Among the texts that accompanied the play were verses from the book of *Genesis* (Ch. 15, vs 18–21), the covenant between Abraham and God which gave the theatrical event political significance, especially during the 1980s when the right-wing government policy-makers tended toward a vision of "Greater Israel".

[48] Meizlish, note 3, 14. In 1983 their numbers reached 11,000. The first half of the 1990s have seen a rise in the number of *baalei teshuva* (no precise numbers available).

the way) using a Freudian interpretation, principally the distinction between the "death" of the individual personality "necessitated" by religious life, and that of a "free", secular way of life:

> The ritual tool symbolizing the spirit of the group is the totem, at which are directed all the commandments and prohibitions connected with the ceremony. In this case, the hen is the totem and the taboo concerning what is permitted or forbidden relates to it. It is a father figure, a god, authority, the manifestation of all these fundamentals [...] the spirit of the totem that is assimilated into the body of the believer and becomes part of him. The believer can discharge the totem, or reject it. He can continue to identify with the totem until death. Assimilation in this case means identification. Rejection is non-identification. If the players/believers go all the way in the direction of identification, they will also have to accept, during the process of assimilation, the fact of the death of the totem within themselves. They must either die or cease the ceremony. In other words: *the religious ritual is a form of death* (emphasis mine, D.U.), the death of the personality and its entry into an accumulated situation that is locked in and sealed. Another possibility is to cease the ritual in order to preserve a situation in which life flows freely without predetermined fixed borders.[49]

The main part of the event takes place at its end, during which the spectators "are programmed" to choose rejection of the religious ritual, by rejecting death of the individual personality. To achieve this, a process of "deconstruction" of the ritual act is suggested, aided by the verses that have accompanied the play: "Everything spoken by the actors has been taken from various holy scriptures. The pieces will be collected together and used according to existing conditions on the spot at any moment. The text is not fixed." (*ibid.* 28) The slaughter of the hen is particularly hard to take, carried out according to all the requirements of the laws of kosher slaughtering. A tray, bowl for the blood, chopping board, knife – all the accessories of ritual slaughter are provided. The scene mainly emphasizes the contrast between the secular and religious viewpoints and rejects any illusion of compromise.

> The man/son says: "this is our atonement", and slaughters the hen [...]. The audience appears to belong to the community of those who have totally lost their way, and the standard slaughter procedure may be interpreted by them as inhumane, and possibly is so from their viewpoint. However, as one knows, between humane thinking and kosher slaughtering or any other ritual act [...] any similarity is purely

---

[49] Amir Orian, *The Cheder [room] Theatre. A New Definition of a Theatrical Term: "Dinner"*, Tel Aviv, 1985, 24–5. (Hebrew)

coincidental [...] The women (proselytes, D.U.) are in fact given the task of directing the secular audience's attention to the more acceptable and convenient characteristics. They are charged with pimping for religion. (*ibid.* 32)

The secular theatre, in these and similar plays, offers the audience a means of auto-immunization against *teshuva*. The secular approach holds the view of sober and independent confrontation with reality and rejects religion as a totalitarian authority. The conflict between religious and secular texts is thus mainly reflected in either the need for such texts or the open rejection of any authority that could be termed "parental".

A Lack of Paternal Affection

Freud perceived a belief in God and religion as a fixated longing for the all-protective father figure, an expression of a desire for help. Psychoanalysis, in contrast, aims at helping one to rely only on one's own strength, intelligence and skills. Freud clarified his ideas in one of his later lectures:

> [...] it is easy to understand how it is that the comforting promises of protection and the severe ethical commands are found together with the cosmogeny. For the same individual to whom the child owes its own existence, the father (or, more correctly, the parental function which is composed of the father and the mother) has protected and watched over the weak and helpless child, exposed as it is to all the dangers which threaten in the external world; in its father's care it felt itself safe. Even the grown man, though he may know that he possesses greater strength, and though he has greater insight into the dangers of life, rightly feels that fundamentally he is just as helpless and unprotected as he was in childhood and that in relation to the external world he is still a child. Even now, therefore, he cannot give up the protection which he has enjoyed as a child. But he has long ago realized that his father is a being with strictly limited powers and by no means endowed with every desirable attribute. He therefore looks back to the memory-image of the overrated father of his childhood, exalts it into a Deity, and brings it into the present and into reality. The emotional strength of this memory-image and the lasting nature of his need for protection are the two supports of his belief in God.[50]

Changing one's religious beliefs may have causal links with the family history of the proselytes. The choice of God, with or without the

---

[50] Sigmund Freud, "A Philosophy of Life", *New Introductory Lectures on Psycho-Analysis*, trans. W.J. Sprott, London, The Hogarth Press, 1949, 208–9.

mediation of a proselytizer, in many instances effectively provides a parental substitute. In Israeli culture such a choice of "parent" contrasts utterly with the "secular parents" [the first and second generations of Jewish settlers in Israel] who have abandoned the religious path and Jewish tradition. One interesting expression of this is exemplified in Yariv ben-Aharon, son of Yitzhak ben-Aharon. Yitzhak was one of the leaders of the Kibbutz Ha'Meuchad Movement and the Zionist-Socialist Worker's Movement. Yariv criticizes his father's exchange of Judaism for socialism and has returned to the perception of the world and the study (albeit without fulfilling the *mitzvot* [commandments incumbent upon Jews to perform]) of the Jewish texts of his "grandfather". In a novel he wrote, Yariv describes this conflict:

> Peleg wonders: Did his father, who in his heart abolished the Diaspora, banish at the same moment God from the land? Did he distance God from his son in order to rule him with his own god of integrity, or did all this happen simply to distance him from the God of his grandfather?[51]

This pattern includes the "grandfather" figure employed by Rabbi Benji Levene from Mea Shearim. By using such a figure, Levene circumvents the father figure who has become secular and "returns" the secular spectator to the grandfather he may have had. Other proselytizers cultivate the authoritative characteristics of a goodly religious father figure.[52] In contrast to such figures are the prominent caricatures of frightening and even emasculating father figures in such secular plays as *In Reverse* and *Dinner*.

Yossef Bar-Yossef remembers how his ultra-Orthodox father, the writer Yehoshua Bar-Yossef, looked before he became an apostate: "I remember him dimly, wearing a long coat, hat, beard, sidelocks. I myself had already spent two years studying in a *cheder*."[53] The father, newly secular, worked for a newspaper and the family moved to live in the Socialist-Zionist Borochov neighbourhood of Tel Aviv. Yossef was transferred from the Jerusalem *cheder* to a school in Borochov. Like the character of the young girl Leah in *Boochie*, he too mumbled "there is no God", to see whether the skies would tremble. His mother remained religious.

---

[51] Yariv Ben-Aharon, *Peleg*, Tel Aviv, Ophir, 1993, 70. See also: 97–98. (Hebrew)

[52] Yassif, note 17, 144, introducing a sermon by Yagen which brings two father figures into confrontation: one, ridiculous, a secular father who is a professor ("threshold guardian") and his son who disparages him; the other, a noted rabbi whose son respects and honours him.

[53] Emanuel Bar-Kedma, "About People who Wasted their Lives", interview with Yossef Bar-Yossef, *Yediot Aharonot*, 24 November 1989.

The child grew up between these two worlds, eventually joining Hashomer Hatzair [a left wing Zionist movement]. "My statement is not, against religion or secularism," explains the playwright, "for between the extremes of religious law practiced by the father, and the mendacious frivolity of the son, there are other ways of existence. As a religious and a secular being, this time I chose a conflict. If there is any statement here at all, it is about the seriousness of both sides. Each side needs to know that it pays a price, for it chooses its own side and not the other."[54]

At one of the turning points in *Boochie*, the protagonist says (in amazement or irony or both): "I really will return to the fold one day." (*ibid.* 95) His *teshuva* is linked to his confused relationship with his sick and dying ultra-Orthodox father. Boochie, who has got into bad company, left his parents' home twelve years ago and has now returned, afraid of his pursuing creditors. He wants his inheritance as well as to solve his relationship with his father. Bar-Yossef explains: "My play about the Orthodox is about a son seeking his father's love."[55] The play features many aspects of father–son relationships, particularly that between Boochie and his father, but also between Boochie and his own son, as well as between Boochie's father Eliyahu and his father. The various comparisons heighten the gap. Eliyahu's father says about Eliahu that "he knows what he's doing, you can rely on him," (*ibid.* 97) and Boochie reacts sorrowfully: "my father never said anything like that to me." (*ibid.*) And, following this line of thought, Boochie speaks about his own son: "I've left the children. A week ago my son stood opposite me with a breadknife, like this! You remember? Like I stood opposite you, with a breadknife!" (*ibid.* 99)

The father–son relationships in *Boochie* attain a "theological" dimension when Boochie's brother-in-law, Nissan, explains why the creation of the world by God is preferable to Darwin's theory of evolution: "Why choose an ape father when one can choose our Father in Heaven? It's true that a great and terrible father is more difficult; the more possessions one has the more one worries. But does anyone throw out his possessions because of the difficulty?" (*ibid.* 69) In this way, he also bestows upon Eliyahu his father-in-law as "a great and terrible father" – a sort of god-like image. And indeed, Boochie recalls resentfully, "when did he ever tell us such stories when we were kids? When did he ever hold our hands?" (*ibid.* 85) "When my skullcap fell off I was afraid he'd hear it in his room. A disaster." (*ibid.* 92) "We never talked," he tells his father sorrowfully, "you only asked me: Where did you pray? Now too. I'm not a small child any longer. Your father said about you: 'you can rely on him'. You never ever trusted me. Before I even opened my mouth

---

[54] Sarit Fuchs, "He Returned with No Answer", *Ma'ariv*, 2 November 1984.
[55] Seamus Finnegan, *James Joyce and the Israelites and Dialogues in Exile*, The Netherlands, Harwood Academic Publishers, 1995, 74.

you said: 'go on, start lying!' I lied [...] I deserve a father, any father, don't I? Why me, why is my father my father only together with God, with the synagogue? I don't believe, I can't, simply can't, it's too much for me, you must understand this. I've nowhere to go but to you, not there, not here, only you still remain." (*ibid.* 99) Only death makes peace between them: "When you die you embrace me, dead, only dead can I embrace you." (*ibid.* 100) Bar-Yossef comments on Boochie's *teshuva*: "All the 'conversions' that we witness, are by the nature of things due to a deep *lack.*" (emphasis mine, D.U.)[56] However, religious conversion, in this version, does not heal the pain caused by a father's lack of paternal affection.

In theatre, in its widest sense, two contrasting viewpoints come into conflict: the secular and the religious. The "vocabulary" of this theatre is a restricted one; the characters, arguments and judgements delivered repeat themselves. One particularly prominent feature is the need for a strong father (= god) figure on the one side and a need to free oneself from such a figure on the other side. There are many for whom Judaism is identified with the grandfather from the Diaspora; this may awaken nostalgic yearnings, but also criticism and even aversion or "self-hatred". The father figure who became secular upon his immigration to *Eretz Israel*, plays a central role in this connection. He represents the possibilities of a life unencumbered by any transcendent authority, through negating the illusions found in religion, and affirming the validity of dealing with human reality with all its difficulties, on one's own. It is no coincidence that the proselytizers have much dealing with grandfather–father–son relationships. Uri Zohar "remembers"[57] his grandfather, who perished in the holocaust, "because of those clothes. Because of the skullcap." Although he is "not angry" with his father who became secular, he does note with satisfaction that his father eventually followed in his footsteps and "at the age of 70 chose the *teshuva.*" He praises in particular his own son, "who turned me into a father" and customarily rises in his presence to show respect.

The proselytizers lead their followers, by means of public appearances and gatherings, away from the postmodern world in which there has occurred what Jean-François Lyotard calls an "incredulity regarding meta-narratives",[58] towards a safe reality in which sons need a "father" and such fatherhood is ritually manifested. In contrast, the theatre reinforces the secular identity while uncovering what it perceives as a ridiculous and false path back to Judaism, and the "pitiful weakness" of those who are in need of an authoritative father figure.

---

[56] Hanna Rosenthal, "There is No God – Thank God", *Al Ha'Mishmar*, 2 November 1984.

[57] Dan, note 15.

[58] Jean-François Lyotard, *The Postmodern Condition: A Report on Knowledge*, trans. Geoffrey Bennington and Brian Massumi, Manchester, Manchester University Press, 1984, 46.

CONCLUSION

In the 1980s and 1990s theatre in its widest sense (mainstream, fringe events of a theatrical nature) became an arena for different and opposing ideological conflicts concerning the Jewish identity of Israeli society and culture. The performers of the latter part of the 20th century have also found stages among religious groups, for whom theatrical performance as such is forbidden by religious law.

The growing number of such performances, particularly in the last decade, is a symptom of the increasing rift between the secular and religious. Despite this, however, those voices which use theatre to present their arguments regarding Judaism, do not simply plead for or against it. Playwrights and other theatre practitioners present their different arguments and approaches, and some playwrights even demonstrate ambivalence or, more accurately, a complex standpoint. Shmuel Hasfari, for example, whose plays voice criticism of the ultra-Orthodox (*The Last Secularist*, 1986) and of religious Zionism (*Kiddush*, 1985), in 1983 staged in the "simple theatre" *The Torah will be given at Six* – a commedia dell'arte version of a dramatized page from the Talmud. Outwardly, the satiric purpose is that of mocking the sacred, such as in one of the scenes in which Moses, chancing upon a meeting of Orthodox Jews is received by the *Ashkenazi* rabbis as an Oriental from Egypt whose actual Jewishness is doubtful. In an interview, Hasfari explained his positive approach to the Jewish culture and how his perception differs from that taken by Zionism, which sees Judaism as belonging to the Diaspora and therefore negative:

> We are talking here about a theatre which will express a sort of associative collective burden, arising from a knowledge of Jewish culture and history. For this reason, there is no need to undergo religious conversion, but simply to become knowledgeable. David Ben-Gurion [first Prime Minister and Founder of the State of Israel], succeeded in developing here an entire generation of Tarzans. According to his approach, from the time of Bar-Kochva [leader of the Jewish revolt against the Romans in 135–132 B.C.E.] up to the *Hagana* [Jewish military organization active during the British Mandate from 1921–1948] there were only pogroms. I turned to theatre with the aim of filling in this gap and illuminating these 1500 years of "darkness".[1]

---

[1] Yaron Barak, "Jewish Theatre with Social Involvement", *Zo Ha'Derech*, 16 November 1983. (Hebrew)

An intellectual approach to the search characterizes some of these theatre practitioners who experimented in "Jewish theatre", particularly in the 1970s and 1980s. They include Yaakov Raz, Danny Horowitz, Yossi Yzraely and the Theatre Company of Jerusalem. They are all seeking the common "deep" structure to their own Jewishness and existence as secular Israelis. Yaakov Raz notes: "I want to reach both the personal deep structures and those of my Jewish-Israeli environment."[2] Their quest recoils from any sort of religious-Jewish reality, and particularly the model of the Diaspora experience of the Jewish *shtetl* [small town] in Eastern Europe. This standpoint leads them to all-inclusive, considered formulas, and to far-reaching adaptations of Jewish texts. The tensions between close/distant in these adaptations are also recognisable in the borrowing from other traditions, such as the Japanese theatre, while ridiculing traditional Jewish signs and elements as well as harnessing Jewish sources for other purposes (political, feminist). Danny Horowitz's comments are typical of the ambivalent attitude to Jewish "materials":

> There are so many high walls between the potential audience and these Jewish materials, that we most certainly did not do this for our own convenience. There is a genuine attempt here to use the materials, which are very personal and important to us, but they are not taken for granted. In other words, there is something that is not taken for granted due to the distance between us, as non-religious people living in Israel of the 1970s and 1980s, and between the materials which are four or five hundred years old and have an intrinsic power. Not only do they belong to an earlier period, but they are bound up in a sort of world vision which has never been ours, such as the religious one. (*ibid.*, 88)

Yossi Yzraely's manifesto "Towards a Jewish Theatre – Preliminary Guidelines" relates less to its Jewish content than to "refining" the tangible characteristics of traditional Jewish culture, and the choice of Jewish concepts (in this particular case concepts from the Kabbala of Rabbi Yitzhak Lurie and the Hassidic Kabbala), particularly those of *Shevira* [destruction in all worlds including the divine] and *Tikkun* [the repair of such destruction], which have constituted the principles of Jewish mystic religious faith from the 16th century on. Disassociating these religious principles from fulfilling the commandments which serve the religious individual in repairing the flaw in Creation and returning everything to its original place, enables Yzraely to present his

---

[2] Ruth Blumert, "Two Dialogues", Bamah 104, 1985, 91. (Hebrew)

Judaism in a general way which suits his secularity and theatrical world vision:

Theatre as Longing

Theatre itself – the chasing after reality, the desperate attempt to conquer it or the foolish attempt to rule it via imitation or an illusion of its realization – is an expression of longing. Longing for the unattainable, ungrasped reality.

Jewish theatre must be developed not as an attempt to realise reality, but as a longing for such reality.

Longing and Fear of Missed Opportunity

The situation of *Shevira* is a constant one for the system. The existential, or theatrical, tension persists between the longing for *Tikkun* – of man and the world – and the fear of missing the opportunity that accompanies the journey towards such *Tikkun*. The longing for the unattainable *Tikkun* and the fear of failing the impossible mission lie at the heart of Jewish theatre.[3]

The majority of Yzraely's "Jewish" plays, like those based upon the literary works of S. Y. Agnon and others from Hassidic sources such as Rabbi Nahman of Braslav, lack contextual semiotic signs that anchor the work against an east-European Jewish background which supports the adapted sources. Yzraely uses theatre as a means of dialogue with the Jewish culture:

The older I get, the more new questions that arise regarding the culture in which I live; or, more accurately – next to which I live, for I am not part of the great Hassidic tradition. It is completely strange and alien to me. When I encounter the tales of Braslav [in the play *The Seven Beggars*, 1979, adapted from the tales of Rabbi Nahman of Braslav, D.U.], I am faced with two possibilities: I can analyze the material, explain it from a historical or literary viewpoint, I can love it with all my heart but it still remains beyond my reach. If I want to enter into it, I must dive into the sea, become a religious man [...] The second possibility is that of theatre. [...] This time [...] I am seeking a personal solution to my existence as an alternative to religion. This does not mean that theatre is religion – absolutely not; but by means of the theatre I am able to create a connection with such matters not as a spectator but as a participant, and that is a tremendous difference.[4]

---

[3] Yossi Yzraely, "Towards a Jewish Theatre – Preliminary Guidelines", *Iton 77*, 59, December 1984, 46. (Hebrew)
[4] Michael Ohad, "Times of Redemption", *Ha'Aretz*, 21 September 1979. (Hebrew)

Yehoshua Sobol has a particularly interesting view of his own
Jewish identity as an Israeli. Outwardly there is some similarity between
him and a fiercely anti-religious playwright such as Yigal Even-Or
(*Fleischer*, 1993), except that Even-Or focuses his struggle against the religious on specific subjects and does not consolidate any all-encompassing
viewpoint. Sobol has been dealing with Judaism in all its aspects for the
last three decades, examining them by means of different tools: first,
using satire (*Status Quo Vadis*, 1973, *Repentance*, 1977) and later in plays
examining Israeli reality and history. Since the production of *Wars of
the Jews* (1981), a play about the destruction of the Second Temple, Sobol
has turned the tension between his Jewishness and his Israeliness into
a central theme in both his own original works and those which he has
translated. His background in philosophy is notable in his approach,
which is influenced by the traditions of the Jewish Enlightenment.
He adopts from Judaism those same values, images and historical events
which he perceives to be of a positive nature, while rejecting and criticizing its darker sides of destructive, extremist nationalism, of superstition and of the religious political establishment.

Sobol uses the period of the Second Temple as a model for
a destructive society, and he warns against the fact (particularly in
Jerusalem Syndrome, 1987) that Israeli society is attempting to adopt this
model, which has two paths: that of Orthodoxy, demanding that the
State's citizens be cut off from all that is enlightened and liberal; and that
of self-destruction, of extreme Jewish nationalism. Sobol, seen by religious circles as "a Jew-hating Israeli", deals in his plays with figures on
the legitimate border of Judaism, such as the anti-Semitic Jewish philosopher Otto Weininger in *Soul of a Jew* (1982), and he dedicates his play *Solo*
(1991) to Baruch Spinoza, a Jewish philosopher rejected by the Jewish
community of Amsterdam:

> My strong identification is with Spinoza, for he is the archetype of the
> non-religious Jew [...] I too am a Jew in essence but not in religion [...]
> Spinoza, who is post-post modern, speaks way above the heads of those
> who convert to ultra-Orthodoxy in our times; he speaks to the individ-
> ual who will emerge after this stage of retreat to religion, that leads to
> nationalism and the hatred of others, has ended.[5]

Many secular playwrights, particularly in the last decade,
demonstrate a sort of contradiction between the desire to create a dialogue with their Jewish heritage and their rejection of the religious Jews
themselves, and particularly the establishment which represents them.

---

[5] Aviva Saltzman, "Swimming against the Stream", *Davar*, 7 October 1991. (Hebrew)

These playwrights include Chonni Hameagel, the Jewish, anti-religious multimedia artist and Performance creator. Hameagel comes from a Rabbinical family, and is the youngest son of a family "blessed with many children". He studied at a *cheder* [religious elementary school] but during his youth he rebelled against religion. He makes use of many Jewish materials and is fond of *hazzanut* [prayer accompanied by song and melody]. However, the Jewish religion "sickens" him, due to its texts, "the immorality of the Torah", and in particular because it humiliates women, whom he enshrines in his works within the Holy Ark of the synagogue.

The approach of secular Israeli playwrights to their Jewishness as a spiritual way of life differing from their secular world (such as meditation or the Hare Krishna cult) can also be learned from the "autobiographic" play *Tshuva* (Repentance) (1997) written by a hesitant convert to ultra-Orthodoxy; a young playwright by the name of Nuriel Tobias. Tobias's first attempt at religious conversion, in an ultra-Orthodox *yeshiva*, was unsuccessful and he left after two months. Five years later he returned to religion via a *yeshiva* belonging to the Braslav Hassidim movement in Jerusalem. During this attempt, which lasted four months in a small and somewhat run-down *yeshiva*, whose pupils were all religious converts, rejecting society – delinquents and the mentally retarded, he underwent some very unusual experiences. He saw the path of prayer and daily gatherings as providing a highly charged emotional experience. The pupils perceived their Rabbi as a father figure, which indeed he may have been. Following this period, Tobias returned to his secular home and cast off all the trappings of the religious world.

Nuriel Tobias exemplifies the intermediary moving between the two worlds. He visits (twice) the world in which he seeks an intrinsic holiness, but his sojourn there is disappointing and the visits only serve to reveal what he sees as the uncleanliness of the holy world. His play gives expression to a narcissistic personality, seeking purity and meaning in a world in which he himself is at the centre. The play tends toward the "anthropological", a visit to the religious community; it is principally a text, one among others, aimed at revealing the "truth" behind the religious figure – the emptiness, idleness, and the quashed and frustrated sexuality. Beyond all of this the play encounters us with the spiritual distress of a secular youth, in his restless and truncated search for happiness and peace of mind in a post-modern world.

Among those from the religious community who turn to theatrical activity, a clear tension can be felt between the lack of any Jewish theatrical traditions, and even the prohibition of such, and their desire to initiate a dialogue with Israeli culture, in which theatre is still to be found at the top of the model of Pierre Bourdieu's, "hierarchy of legitimacies".[6] Most of these theatre practitioners (Zippora Luria, Rabbi Baruch Brenner, Rabbi Benji Levene) see theatre as a strategy which introduces their world vision to secular society, although they cannot dispense with their religious reservations. Michal Guvrin, a theatre practitioner who is traditionally observant, warns against the "translation of Jewish tradition into structural tools, taken from other ritual-theatrical sources [which] may empty them of their essential meaning."[7] Justifying theatre among the religious is instrumental. It serves to persuade the secular community regarding Jewish "truth"; and, as we have seen, to assist in the struggle by religious women within their own community to change their status. Yehuda Moraly, a *baal teshuva*, researcher and theatre practitioner, perceives theatre as a solution to the problem of assimilation:

> In these times a sort of "pink holocaust" is taking place [...] People are simply entering mixed marriages, or not bothering to marry at all. This has already been going on for two or three generations! *A contented people is being destroyed with a smile* [emphasis mine, D.U.]. [...] The only way to speak to this people is through art, in the theatre, and mainly – via the cinema. And I am not talking about just one individual piece of work, but about a *flood of brilliant pieces* that will enrich an open-mouthed audience, with the thought: Hey, perhaps there is something to Judaism after all.[8]

Among other religious groups theatre does not serve for a dialogue but, rather, as a means of attacking the secular culture and proving its worthlessness, particularly to audiences of the traditionally observant. The 1980s and 1990s have seen the development of a popular religious culture of theatrical-preachers who make use of dramatic tools to disseminate Judaism and preach its principles to audiences of mainly oriental origin. These theatrical sermons, which are on the increase (also on audio and video-cassettes), adapt the art at the top of Bourdieu's model to suit audiences who have never been to the theatre. Such "lowering" of the theatre also serves a political role in this case, confusing the artistic hierarchy, and questioning the social hierarchy which lies behind it. The enlightened, secular community, which is mainly of western origin, and for whom the theatre is a specially chosen gathering place,

---

[6] Pierre Bourdieu, Luc Boltanski, Robert Castel and Jean Claude Chamboredon and Dominique Shnapper, *Photography: A Middle-brow Art*, trans. Shaun Whiteside, Stanford, California, Stanford University Press, 1990, 95–8.

[7] Michal Guvrin, "The Jewish Ritual as a Genre of 'Holy Theatre'", *Judaism and Art*, David Cassuto (ed.), Institute for Judaism and Contemporary Thought, Bar Ilan University, 1989, 263. (Hebrew)

[8] Interview: Zippora Luria, "Bringing Back the Miracle", *Dimui*, 5–6, 1993, 11. (Hebrew)

finds itself being attacked by its "own" artistic tools for being a hegemony in Israeli society. These performances constitute a battle cry by popular religion against the *Ashkenazi* elite who have converted secularism into a sort of religion. There has been increasing awareness of this conflict since the parliamentary turnabout in the 1996 elections, which saw the rise of several powerful religious groups, particularly those representatives of oriental religious Judaism.

The decreased interest taken by secular theatre practitioners in the last decade in a dialogue with their Jewish heritage matches the religious community's tendency towards seclusion, as can also be seen in their use of theatre as a means of expression within their own community and for their own needs, as if they have renounced any hope of dialogue. Even the stereotyping displayed by the secular toward the religious – going so far as "self-hatred", finds its match in the *Ashkenazi* negative intellectual stereotype depicted in the popular religious "theatre". The future relations between the two communities, it would seem, will not be determined in the theatre, but in the political "field"; nonetheless, the continued conflict between secular playwrights who turn secularism into a religion, and the religious groups who also use theatrical means to voice their protests over the advantages of a hegemonic group, would appear to promise that a continued debate of "public thought" over the issue of the Jewishness of Israeli society will remain an important subject in Israeli theatre well into the coming century.

GLOSSARY

Aliyah rishonah: first wave of Jewish immigration, 1882–1903
Ashkenazi: of European/western origin
Baal teshuva: member of a group of secular Jews who have converted to Orthodox Judaism
Beth Midrash: a place for Torah study
Chalutz: pioneer
Cheder: religious elementary school
Chiloni: secular
Chozer b'tshuva: returnee to the religious fold
Dvekut: devoutness. Devotion to God is considered by Hassidism to be the principal value in man's life in all stages of religious work
Eretz Israel: the Land of Israel
Fellah: Arab agricultural labourer
Gematria: a form of numerology
Goy: non Jew
Gush Emunim: the movement of the Zionist-religious settlers in the occupied territories
Halacha: the Jewish religious law
Haliza: release from a widow's obligation to marry the brother of her late husband
Haskala: the Jewish Enlightenment movement
Hashomer Hatzair: a leftwing Zionist movement
Hazzanut: prayer accompanied by song and melody
Kapota: coat
Knesset: Israeli parliament
Lehi: one of the Jewish underground organisations, prior to the establishment of the State, which fought mainly against the British
Mamzer: one born of an illicit, e.g. an adulterous union
Midrash: laws and legends studied from the Bible
Minyan: quorum for prayer
Mitzvot: religious commandments incumbent upon Jews to perform
Sephardi: of oriental origin
Shofar: holy ram's horn
Shomer mitzvot: one who observes the religious commandments
Shtetl: Jewish township in Central and Eastern Europe prior to the Second World War

Shulchan Aruch: codification of Jewish law compiled by Joseph Caro, first printed in 1565

Streimel: fur-brimmed hat

Tallith: ritual prayer shawl

Talmud: the largest body of Jewish law from the 3rd to 6th centuries A.D.

Tefillin: phylacteries

Teshuva: the return to total observance of the Jewish Law

Tsitsit: fringes on the ritual prayer shawl

Yeshiva: college for Torah study

Yishuv: the Jewish community in Palestine during the period of the British Mandate

Zaddik: Hassidic rabbi and leader

BIBLIOGRAPHY

Jewish Religion in Israel

Books:

Janet Aviad, *Return to Judaism: Religious Renewal in Israel*, Chicago and London, The University of Chicago Press, 1983.

Benjamin Beit-Hallahmi, *Despair and Deliverance: Private Salvation in Contemporary Israel*, Albany, State University of New York Press, 1992.

Eliezer Ben-Rafael, *Ethnicity, Religion and Class in Israeli Society*, Cambridge, Cambridge University Press, 1991.

Tamar El-Or, *Educated and Ignorant: Ultra-Orthodox Jewish Women and their World*, Boulder, Colorado, Lynne Rienner, 1994.

Shlomit Levy, Hanna Levinsohn and Elihu Katz, *Beliefs, Observances, and Social Relations among Israeli Jews*, Jerusalem, Louis Guttman Israel Institute of Applied Social Research, 1993.

Charles S. Liebman, Eliezer Don-Yehiya, *Religion and Politics in Israel*, Bloomington, Indiana University Press, 1984.

Liebman (ed.), *Religious and Secular: Conflict and Accommodation between Jews in Israel*, Jerusalem, Keter, 1990.

Zvi Sobel, *Jewish Fundamentalism in Comparative Perspective: Religion, Ideology and the Crisis of Modernity*, New York, New York University Press, 1993.

Sobel, Beit-Hallahmi (eds.), *Tradition, Innovation, Conflict: Jewishness and Judaism in Contemporary Israel*, Albany, State University of New York Press, 1991.

Articles:

Menachem Friedman, 'The State of Israel as a Theological Dilemma", in: *The Israeli State and Society: Boundaries and Frontiers*, Baruch Kimmerling (ed.), Albany, State University of New York, 1989.

Baruch Kurzweil, "Notes on Hebrew Literature", in: *What Is Jewish Literature?* Hanna Wirth-Nesher (ed.), Philadelphia, Jewish Publication Society, 1994.

Aviezer Ravitzki, "Exile in the Holy Land: the Dilemma of Haredi Jewry", "Israel: State and Society, 1948–1988", *Studies in Contemporary Jewry*, Vol. 5, 1989.

Yossef Shilhav, "The Haredi Ghetto: the Theology behind the Geography", *Contemporary Jewry*, Vol. 10, No. 2, 1989.

Naomi Struch, Shalom H. Schwartz, "Intergroup Aggression: its Predicators and Distinctness from In-group Bias", *Journal of Personality and Social Psychology*, Vol. 56, No. 3, 1989.

Theatre in Israel

Books:

Glenda Abramson, *Modern Hebrew Drama*, New York, St. Martin's Press, 1979.

Linda Ben-Zvi (ed.), *Theater in Israel*, The University of Michigan Press, 1996.

Seamus Finnegan (ed.), *James Joyce and the Israelites and Dialogues in Exile*, The Netherlands, Harwood Academic Publishers, 1995.

Mendel Kohansky, *The Hebrew Theatre: Its First Fifty Years*, Jerusalem, Israel Universities Press, 1969.

Emanuel Levy, *The Habima Israel's National Theatre, 1917–1977*, New York, Columbia University Press, 1979.

Shimon Levy, *Here, There and Everywhere*, Brighton, Sussex Academic Press, 1996.

Gershon Shaked, *Hebrew Historical Drama in the Twentieth Century*, Jerusalem, Bialik Institute, 1970.

Dan Urian (ed.), "Palestinians and Israelis in the Theatre", *Contemporary Theatre Review*, Vol. 3, No. 2., Harwood Academic Publishers, 1995.

Dan Urian, *The Arab in Israeli Drama and Theatre*, trans. Naomi Paz, The Netherlands, Harwood Academic Publishers, 1997.

Articles:

Haim Nagid, "Israel", in: *World Encyclopedia of Contemporary Theater*, London, Routledge, 1994.

Freddie Rokem, "Ideology and Archetypal Patterns in the Israeli Theatre", *Theatre Research International*, Vol. 13, No. 2, 1988.

Rokem, "Memory and History: 'The Soul of a Jew' By Jehoshua Sobol", *Assaph*, No. 5, 1989.

Eli Rozik, "The Language of the Jews and the Jewish Theatre", *Theatre Research International*, Vol. 13, No. 2, Summer 1988.

Chaim Shoham, "Here and There: the Israeli Playwright and his Jewish Shadow", *MHL*, Fall-Winter 1984.

Shoshana Weitz, "Theatre and Society in Israel", *Theatre Research International*, Vol. 13, No. 2, Summer 1988.

INDEX

Other titles in the Contemporary Theatre Studies series:

This book is part of a series. The publisher will accept continuation orders which may be cancelled at any time and which provide for automatic billing and shipping of each title in the series upon publication. Please write for details.